Making Traditional Pull-Along Toys in Wood

Making Traditional Pull-Along Toys in Wood

Alan & Gill Bridgewater

 Sterling Publishing Co., Inc.   New York

Library of Congress Cataloging-in-Publication Data

Bridgewater, Alan.
    Making traditional pull-along toys in wood / Alan & Gill
Bridgewater.
       p.   cm.
    Includes index.
    ISBN 0-8069-8216-0
    1. Wooden toy making.   I. Bridgewater, Gill.   II. Title.
TT174.5.W6B738   1992
745.592—dc20   91-40795
                                                  CIP

10 9 8 7 6 5 4 3 2

Published in 1992 by Sterling Publishing Company, Inc.
387 Park Avenue South, New York, N.Y. 10016
© 1992 by Alan & Gill Bridgewater
Distributed in Canada by Sterling Publishing
% Canadian Manda Group, P.O. Box 920, Station U
Toronto, Ontario, Canada M8Z 5P9
Distributed in Great Britain and Europe by Cassell PLC
Villiers House, 41/47 Strand, London WC2N 5JE, England
Distributed in Australia by Capricorn Link Ltd.
P.O. Box 665, Lane Cove, NSW 2066
Manufactured in the United States of America
All rights reserved

Sterling ISBN 0-8069-8216-0

Dedication

We would like to dedicate this book to all the anonymous toymakers of the past who have inspired us in our work. For some, toymaking was their livelihood; for others, it was a parental necessity. Many were self-taught, naïve, and humble, but the pleasure they took in their work shines through!

Acknowledgments

We are indebted to the many individuals who helped to make this book a reality.

First of all, we would like to acknowledge our sons. Thank you, Glyn, for working so hard. Thank you, Julian, for sorting out many of the tools.

In addition, we would like to thank Tracy A. Emmison for all the wonderful Humbrol paints, C. N. for "test-flying" the airplane toy, and our editor, Laurel Ornitz, for all her courteous and friendly beyond-the-call-of-duty help.

CONTENTS

Color section follows page 32.

INTRODUCTION

Pull-along toys on wheels are just as popular now as they were 2,000 or so years ago when they were first in use. The popularity of wheeled toys is borne out by examples having been found as far apart in time and space as ancient Egypt (Illus. 1), Greece, and Rome in the East, and in just about every place and period in the Western world.

Illus. 1. Top: Egyptian wooden horse (originally on wheels), made about the time of the Roman occupation. Bottom: Detail from a fifth-century Attic vase, showing a child playing with a wheeled toy.

Every country and period has its own characteristic type of toy. In sixteenth-century Germany, the toymakers favored naïvely carved horses on wheels (Illus. 2). In eighteenth-century Poland, there were beautiful hand-whittled shepherdesses, complete with sheep, all mounted on a wheeled base (Illus. 3). And nineteenth-century German toymakers produced all manner of carved, turned, and painted toys with wheels—everything from trains, wagons, and trucks to rocking-baby carts, soldiers on horses and huge boats (Illus. 4–6).

This book is jam-packed with exciting toy-making projects: a pull-along cow with a moving head and tail, a duck that bobs up and down as it is pulled along, a horse that swings, a sit-on tugboat, a Noah's Ark full of animals, a sausage dog, a rabbit on a cycle, an old woman who lives in a shoe, a ladybug on ball-wheels—all wonderful, vibrant, exciting examples of wooden pull-along action toys. I say "action" because, as well as the toys being exciting and dynamic in the sense that they are on wheels, each and every toy in this collection has a secondary movement or function. The rabbit's legs whizz round and round as he cycles along, the airplane has a flick-

Illus. 2. German sixteenth-century carved wooden pull-along horse—23½″ high. Note the free-turning wheels and the axle pins.

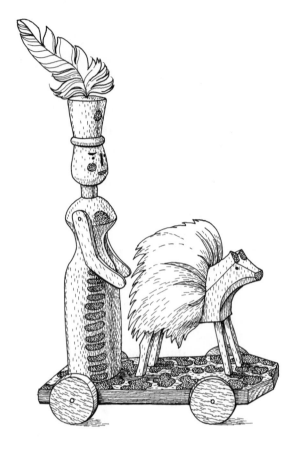

around propeller, the elephant will nod his head when his tail is pressed down, the pull-along ladies dance round and round, and so on. In addition to being mounted on wheels, all the toys variously swing, trundle, dance, bob, pedal, twirl, whirl, and roll.

The range of movement is made even more exciting because, from toy to toy, we use all manner of wheel-and-axle variations and combinations. There are plump wooden wheels, bright shiny plastic wheels, bead-wheels, ball-wheels, and dowel-pivoted roller-wheels. There are fastened wheels on free-turning axles, wheels that spin on fastened axles, ball-wheels mounted in holes, and casters half hidden from view. There are shafts, pendulums, cams, springs, cranks, friction-drive bearings, and pivot levers. There are wheels on pins, wheels on pivots, wheels on mushroom-stub axles, and much more.

These pull-along wooden toys can be as exciting for the toymaker as for the child who eventually gets to play with them. From the toymaker's viewpoint, we see this book as being more than instructions for making specific toys; we see it as being an introduction—an open door—to woodworking in general and wooden toymaking in particular. We describe how to turn wheels, figures, and spindles on the lathe, how to use the scroll saw, how to

Illus. 3. Polish—eighteenth century?—shepherdess-with-sheep toy—turned, whittled, and painted.

Illus. 4. German (Erzgebirge) painted wooden train, 1850.

10

bore holes with the drill press, and how to saw, plane, cut, fret, glue, paint, and finish. We describe the complete designing-and-crafting process—from first considering the tool and material implications of making a particular toy, right through to applying the last dab of varnish and tying on the pull-cord.

The toys have been carefully chosen and designed so that each project will add to the sum total of your woodworking and toymaking skills and experience. We have also gone out of our way to suggest all manner of exciting variations and modifications. This is not to say that you need to work through the whole gamut of techniques presented for every project, but, rather, that you should consider the various working methods, and then, based on all the possibilities, select the approach that best suits you.

If you have any questions about tools, techniques, terms, or materials, the section that follows should be especially helpful. Not to worry if you are a beginner, because, with the detailed instructions and accompanying illus-

Illus. 6. Left: A modern copy of an old German (Erzgebirge) toy—turned, whittled, and pivoted. The pendulum is swung to set the seesaw in motion. Right: A Turkish horse soldier—German (Salzburg), nineteenth century, carved and painted.

trations, there's no reason why you shouldn't be able to make a wonderful range of pull-along toys.

From the child's viewpoint, all the toys in this book have been rigorously tested to the point of destruction by the best of all judges—children themselves!

What child—or adult, for that matter—will be able to resist a duck that waddles, a ladybug with a curious roll-around body, or any of the other moving pull-along delights?

Okay folks, no more praise and promises—now is the time to roll up your sleeves, get out your tools, sort through your supply of wood, and set out your paints and brushes. Mmmm, there's nothing quite like the pungent tang of freshly cut beech, and the smooth zip of a sharp blade biting through the wood!

Good luck and happy toymaking.

Illus. 5. German (Erzgebirge) nineteenth-century toy. When a string is pulled, the mother's foot sets the cradles in motion.

TOOLS, TECHNIQUES, TIPS, AND TERMS

A Toymaker's Glossary

Acrylic paint A plastic polyvinyl-acetate-type paint that is easy to use, water-based, and quick drying. Acrylics are perfect for toymaking, because they can be used straight from the can, the colors are bright, they dry swiftly, and most important of all, they are nontoxic. As pull-along toys get a lot of handling, it's a good idea to protect the painted surfaces with a couple of coats of yacht varnish.

Ball-wheels Wheels that are made using large pivoted beads or balls. They can be made of wood, rubber, or plastic, or can be in the form of shop-bought casters.

Beam compass Arcs and circles that are too large to be drawn with a two-legged compass are best worked with a beam compass. You can make your own from a length of straight wood. All you do is drill a line of closely spaced holes from one end of the wood to the other; the required radius is set by locating a pivot nail or pin in one selected hole and a pencil in another.

Bearing In the context of toymaking, a bearing is a support, guide, locating block, or containment that holds a turning shaft, axle, or pivot. Bearings need to be free from friction; to this end, wood-to-wood bearings need to be waxed and metal-to-metal bearings greased or oiled.

Beech A heavy, pleasant, hardwood that is perfect for toymaking. Red, orange, or yellow in color, beech turns, saws, and cuts well, and generally takes a good finish. It's a very useful wood for making complex profiles and hard-edged details, such as for dolls, turned spindles, base bearing blocks, axle rods, beads, and wheels.

Between centers In the context of wood turning, the mounting of the workpiece between the forked headstock center and the pointed tailstock center. A technique used for turning dowels, spindles, balls, and long urn-like profiles.

Blank Just about any block, slab, disc, or cylinder of ready-to-work wood.

Bow saw A hand-held saw having an H-shaped wooden frame and a slender, flexible blade that is good for cutting curves in a thin piece of wood.

Bradawl A hand-held spiked tool, used for making starter and center-point holes for screws, drill bits, and the like.

Broomstick dowel A cylindrical wooden dowel or rod. See **Dowel**.

Brushes Brushes come in many shapes, sizes, types, and qualities. There are flat brushes for varnishing, long-haired fine-point brushes for details, broad brushes for large areas of flat paint, and so on. We favor using the soft-haired type, the kind used by watercolorists. If you are using acrylic paints, make sure that you wash your brushes as soon as you have finished with them, dry them well, and store them with their bristles tightly bound with plastic film.

Callipers A two-legged measuring instrument, used for checking sizes and stepping off set measurements. If you have a choice, select one that has a screw adjustment. Wood turners also use double-ended figure-eight callipers.

Cam In a toymaking context, a rotating offset form, or lever, attached to the drive shaft. As the drive shaft turns, so the cam sets some part of the toy in motion.

Carton cardboard Cardboard salvaged from packaging that is very useful for making patterns, models, and templates.

Caster A small swivel, disc, or ball type of wheel, used to achieve fast, easy, smooth, stable, safe, tight-turning movement.

Centers In a wood-turning context, the pivotal points are described as "centers." The forked center is at the left-hand side, or headstock end, of the lathe, whereas the pointed-cup center is at the right-hand side, or tailstock end. If a project is described as being "turned between centers," the workpiece is turned while being held and pivoted between the forked center and the pointed center.

Centering and roughing out Mounting the wood on the lathe and turning the initial cylinder.

The procedure is as follows: Take the square piece of wood and establish the end center-points by drawing crossed diagonals, push or tap the wood onto the pronged drive or headstock center, bring the tailstock center up towards the work and clamp it into position, wind the tailstock center into the wood, adjust the tool rest just below center height so that it is clear of the work, grasp the tool in both hands and steady it on the rest, switch on the power, and run the tool backward and forward along the wood until the initial cylinder is roughed out.

If you are working on a small lathe, it's best to cut the wood down to an octagonal shape before you mount it. See **Roughing out**.

Center-line A line that marks out the center of a symmetrical form or image. In toymaking, there are sometimes two such lines: one that runs from side to side, and another that runs from front to back. The center-lines should cross each other at right angles.

Chuck—a four-jawed screw chuck In wood turning, a device used to hold the workpiece while it is being turned. The four jaws are screwed, in geared unison, towards the center, so as to hold and centralize the workpiece. Although screw chucks are expensive, they are wonderfully efficient and time saving.

Clamps and hold-downs Screw devices used for holding wood while it is being worked or cut. They are variously called C-clamps, strap clamps, hold-downs, and so on. In use, the wood to be clamped is protected with off-cut wasters. See **V-block**.

Close-grained This refers to wood that has narrow annual-growth rings. Such woods are usually good and reliable for toymaking. Always make sure that the wood you choose is splinter-proof and nontoxic when making toys.

Coat-hanger wire Wire salvaged from galvanized coat hangers that is very useful, inexpensive, and easy to obtain.

Compasses A two-legged, hand-held instrument used for drawing circles and arcs. It's best to get the long-legged, multipurpose, screw-operated type. See also **Beam compass** and **Dividers**.

Coping saw A small, hand-held, flexible, bladed frame saw used for cutting curves and profiles. It's the perfect saw for plywood, for cutting out holes, and for working enclosed corners and curves. The inexpensive blades can easily be changed.

Cord, rope, and pull-cord In the context of pull-along toys, the cord, rope, braid, or twine that is used to pull the toy along. For children's delicate hands, it is best to use a braid, rope, or cord that is thick, soft, and covered with cotton, and sold by boat chandlers. Such cord can be obtained in all manner of diameters, qualities, textures, and bright fast colors. The length of the pull-cord is important; it needs to be long enough for the child to be able to control the toy but not so long that it will get tangled or be dangerous. It's a good idea to adjust the length of the cord to suit the toy and the child.

Counterbalance Many small pull-along toys use a counterbalance, usually in the form of a seesaw-like weight or extension that balances or offsets another movement.

Countersink To enlarge the upper part of a hole in timber, metal, etc. so that the head of a bolt or screw can be sunk below the surface.

Craft knife A knife with a short, sharp, strong, easy-to-change blade. We use a good selection of clasp knives, penknives, and scalpels.

Crank A U-shaped bend or kink in a shaft, whereby reciprocating motion is converted to rotary motion or vice versa. In terms of small wooden pull-along toys, cranked axles are used to set some part of the toy in motion.

Cut in In wood turning, this refers to sliding the parting tool or the skew chisel directly into the wood. As a general woodworking term, it is used to describe the act of making an initial cut.

Cutouts The plywood shapes that make up the project, or the sawn shapes as they come off the scroll saw.

Designing The process of working out shapes, structures, forms, functions, and details. We usually draw inspiration from museum originals, modify the details to suit our own needs, make working models from remnants of thin wood, cardboard, and string, make further modifications and adjustments, and then draw up the full-size measured designs.

Dividers A two-legged compasslike instrument used for stepping off measurements. In wood turning, the heavy-duty dividers are set at an exact measurement and the two knife-sharp points are held against the workpiece while it is in motion. The points mark the surface with small cut V-grooves.

Be warned: Beginners are best advised to stop the lathe when using dividers.

Double-sided transparent tape A sticky tape used between smooth, flat, mating surfaces. It's good for holding pieces of plywood together while you are cutting out identical multiple shapes on the scroll saw.

Dowel—broomstick dowel or rod Smooth, machine-turned, cylindrical hardwood is one of the toymaker's most important materials. Dowel is sold in diameters that range from $\frac{1}{8}''$, $\frac{1}{4}''$, and $\frac{3}{8}''$, through to $1''$. The diameters that are greater than $1''$ are usually described as being poles, rods, broomsticks, or rails. Dowel can be used as axle rods, sliced to make wheels, cut into lengths to make roller-wheels, cut and carved and made into limbs, used for glued attachments, and so on. When you are gluing a dowel, cut a groove around or along the part that is to be glued so that excess glue can ooze out of the dowel hole (Illus. 1).

Drafting paper See **Tracing paper**.

Drill chuck In terms of wood turning, a gripping device used at the tailstock end of the lathe for holding and centering drill bits. In use, the workpiece is set in motion and the chuck-held drill is moved forward so as to bore a centralized hole.

Drilling holes In many instances, I prefer to work with an easy-to-use, hand-operated drill. Such a drill takes a good range of bit sizes, is silent, can drill holes quickly, is inexpensive, and, most important of all, is totally controllable. In use, the workpiece is backed with a scrap of wood and secured with a clamp, the angle of the drill is checked by eye or with a try square, and the drill is held and steadied with one hand and set in motion with the other.

Drill press A bench-mounted electric drill used for wood or metal. A drill with a bit-gripping chuck, an adjustable height/angle worktable, and various jig and stop attachments. If you plan on making a lot of toys, having such a drill is very useful.

Drive shaft The main shaft that, by way of cams, levers, and friction-drive wheels, is used to set other parts of the toy in motion.

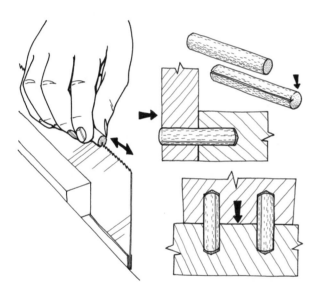

Illus. 1. Dowel peg. Left: Cut a saw slot for the excess glue to ooze out of the joint. Top right: The slot needs to run the full length of the peg; round off the sawn ends with sandpaper. Bottom: Apply glue to the pegs and to all mating faces of the joint.

Dust-free Before you start painting, make sure that the workpiece is free from wood dust and debris. Sweep up the debris, vacuum the surfaces of the workpiece, and then wipe it over with a dampened cloth. Ideally,

painting is done in a dust-free area that has been especially set aside for that purpose.

Enlarging grids See **Gridded working drawing**.

Files Files come in many shapes and sizes; there is everything from fine needle and riffler files through to large two-handed rasps.

Fillers If you need to fill breaks, cavities, and scratches, such as those that occur on the cut edges of some poor-grade multicore plywoods, it's best to use a stable two-tube plastic/resin auto-body filler, one that can be sanded, sawn, and drilled. Avoid using plaster-type fillers as they crumble and are difficult to paint.

Finishing The process of filling, sanding, rubbing down, staining, painting, varnishing, and otherwise bringing the work to a satisfactory structural, textural, and mechanical, and visually exciting, conclusion.

Fit and assemble To put the toy together—to trim to size, fit, apply glue, and fasten with screws, nails, pins, and bolts.

Forstner drill bit A bit designed specifically for boring out flat-bottomed holes in wood. Although Forstner bits are three or four times the price of regular spade or flat drill bits, you can count on them to produce clean-faced, crisp, accurate holes.

Friction-drive In the context of toymaking, a movement achieved by having a turning wheel, belt, band, or roller rubbing against another shaft or wheel. The friction-drive wheel can be set on the same plane as the part to be driven, or it can be set at an angle so as to convert a horizontal movement into a vertical movement.

Friction-fit, or push-fit To fit together two or more components so that one part is a perfect fit within another. For instance, a tenon might be a good friction-fit in a mor-

16

tise, or a dowel might be a perfect fit in a wheel hole or axle bearing.

Glues and adhesives   Although there are many glues and adhesives to choose from, we recommend using PVA (polyvinyl acetate) and/or Super Glue. A ready-to-use and relatively inexpensive glue, PVA is perfect for large joints, attaching dowels, mating flat surfaces, and the like. Although Super Glue is expensive and somewhat tricky to use, it is a good choice when you want to make a small, fast, very strong, dab-and-hold type of joint. See also **Resin glue**.

Gridded working drawing   A drawing or set of plans that has been drawn onto a scaled grid. For example, if the scale of the grid is described as being "four grid squares to 1″," it means that each one of the grid squares can be read off as being a ¼″ unit of measurement. If you want to change the scale, all you do is draw up a larger grid and transfer the image one square at a time.

Hand drill   See **Drilling holes**.

Headstock   In wood turning, the headstock is the power-driven unit at the left-hand end of the lathe. The headstock carries two trust bearings in which the spindle, or mandrel, revolves. The power is supplied to the spindle by means of an electric motor and a drive belt. The spindle has an external screw for chucks and faceplates, and an internal taper for the pronged center.

Inspirational designs and material   Wooden pull-along toys, in museums and shops as well as in manufacturers' literature and old books and magazines, could all be described as inspirational material. It's a good idea to keep a sketchbook/scrapbook and to take note of interesting designs, motifs, patterns, and attachments.

For most of our toys, we drew our inspiration from museum originals. This is not to say that we copied toy designs, but only that by studying forms, movements, profiles, drive mechanisms, designs, and decorations, we gradually came up with new ideas or at least interesting variations on old themes.

Be warned: If you intend to sell the toys you make, be careful not to use copyright material.

Lathe   A woodworking machine for cutting round sections of wood. The wood is pivoted between centers or held in a chuck and spun against a hand-held cutting tool.

Lathe safety   *The lathe is potentially an extremely dangerous piece of equipment.*

Before you switch on the lathe, always:

1. Make sure that the workpiece is well mounted and secure.
2. Turn the work over by hand and make sure that it is clear of the tool rest.
3. Tie back your hair, roll up your sleeves, and generally make sure that you aren't going to get dragged into the equipment.
4. Make sure that children and pets are out of harm's way.

When you have switched on the power, always:

1. Stop the motor or at least slow down before testing with a template, dividers, or callipers.
2. Move the rest well out of the way before sanding.
3. Wear safety glasses.
4. Make sure that your chosen wood is nontoxic.
5. Hold all the tools firmly.
6. Make sure that the cut-off switch is within easy reach.
7. Never reach out over the lathe while it is running.

Note: There are, of course, many more hazards—everything from potentially toxic wood dust to tools falling off shelves and the workpiece flying off the lathe. All you can do is always be wide awake and ready for the unexpected.

Mating faces Surfaces that touch, the area between two touching parts, and two faces that are to be glued together are all described as "mating faces."

Maquette A small working model, or prototype. If, after drawing up the design, you have any doubts at all as to how one part might work or fit in relation to another, then it's best to make a maquette from cardboard or inexpensive wood.

Masking tape A general-purpose paper tape that is especially good for masking off areas when you are painting, holding down working drawings, strapping up work that has been glued, and so on.

Master design The final measured working drawing, the drawing from which the tracings and all other details are taken.

Modifying The process of changing and redesigning some aspect of the project to suit your own needs. If you like the overall idea of a particular toy, but you want, for example, to change its size or the shape of its wheels, the process of changing the design is called "modifying."

Movement The drive mechanism—all the turning, spinning, rolling, swinging, and otherwise moving levers, cams, washers, springs, and strings that go into making up the project.

Multicore plywood When you are making toys, it's important that you always use a best-quality, birch-faced, multicore, or multiveneer, type of plywood. Such a plywood comes in thicknesses ranging from $1/8''$ through $1''$ and is made up from layers that are about $1/16''$ thick. It's cheaper to purchase a whole $48 \times 96''$ sheet rather than small pieces cut to size. In use, best-quality multicore plywood can easily be cut on a scroll saw, with all faces and edges being worked to a smooth and even finish.

Be warned: Cheap-grade "soft-heart" or "coarse center" plies are very difficult to work. The laminations break down and the cut edges are so open-grained that they always need filling.

Naïve, or primitive In the context of this book, these are positive terms used to describe unsophisticated, uninhibited, traditional folk-art toys.

Off-cuts Bits and pieces (remnants) of scrap wood left over from other projects. It's best to use them for small jobs and for making prototypes. Many wood suppliers sell off-cuts.

Painting and painting area When you come to painting, start by making sure that the object to be painted is clean, dry, and free from dust. The actual painting is best done in an area that has been set aside and organized specifically for this purpose. Spend time, prior to painting, carefully setting out all your paints and materials, and considering how the objects are going to be supported when they have been painted. If the toy is to be painted as separate components before it is put together, the items could be hung on a line, placed on a wire rack, or hung from wire hooks, to dry. Ideally, pull-along toys should be rubbed down with the graded sandpapers, given a couple of coats of matt acrylic paint, detailed with a fine-point brush, and varnished.

We favor the use of acrylics because they are "user-friendly." Acrylics dry very quickly, several coats of paint can be applied in a short time, the brushes can be washed in water, the colors are bright, and everything is nontoxic. Of course, oil paints are also bright and they come in a huge range of wonderful colors, but they take days to dry, all the equipment needs to be cleaned with solvents, and, in terms of toxicity, the ingredients of many are suspect. If you are a beginner, it's best to start with acrylics and then to experiment with other types of paint as you go along.

Pencils and pencil-press-transferring We use a soft 2B for designing and tracing, and a hard "H" for pencil-press-transferring. The order of work is as follows: Draw out the full-size master design, take a careful tracing, pencil in the back of the tracing with a 2B pencil, turn the tracing right side up and attach it to the working surface of the wood with tabs of masking tape, and finally rework the traced lines with a hard pencil.

Pilot hole A small guide hole that is drilled prior to inserting a nail or screw, or a drilled hole through which the blade of the scroll saw can be passed.

Pivot In the context of toymaking, a pivot is the point, rod, bolt, rivet, shaft, or dowel on which another part might swing, turn, roll, or otherwise move.

Plane A hand-held tool with an adjustable steel blade, used for smoothing and levelling wood. For toymaking, it's best to use a small, metal bench plane.

Pliers and grips Pliers and grips come in many shapes and sizes. Their uses range from lifting out small nails to snipping and bending wire, fastening small nuts, gripping difficult-to-hold components, and so on. At the very least, you need a pair of long-nosed pliers and a pair of locking grips.

Profiles Any cutout, silhouette, cross section, drawn shape, flat fretted form, or turning might be termed a profile.

Prototype A working model made prior to making the toy. If you aren't quite sure how the toy is going to function, or if you are considering making a few modifications, then you need to sort out potential problems by making a mock-up, or prototype. See also **Maquette.**

Pyrography The art, craft, or process of using an electric penlike tool to burn designs onto/into wood.

Punch A small, hand-held, pointed metal tool used for driving nails into wood. In use, the punch is located on the nail head and struck with a hammer. It's good for making swift center-point holes for screws and drill bits.

Rasps and files Rasps and files come in many shapes and sizes. There's everything from small needle and riffler files, through to large, two-handed, Surform-type plane rasps. Toymakers need a wide selection.

Resin glue A two-tube resin-to-hardener adhesive. It can be tricky to use, so always read the instructions.

Roller-wheels Wheels made in the form of long end-pivoted rollers. They can be made by using large-diameter dowels for the rollers, and small-diameter dowels or brass rods for the pivots.

Roughing out To chop or cut away the waste. In wood turning, roughing out refers to the initial stage of swiftly turning off the waste and achieving a round section of wood. If you are using a small lathe, it's best to establish the end-centers by drawing crossed diagonals, to draw tangents to the diagonals, and finally to remove the bulk of the waste with a plane or drawknife. When using a small lathe, removing the bulk of the waste prior to mounting the wood on the lathe makes the task of turning that much easier and less hazardous (Illus. 2).

Rubbing down Taking the sawn profiles and other sections, and working them to a smooth, ready-to-paint finish. Working well away from the painting area, we usually trim off the corners, edges, and burrs with a plane or chisel, swiftly rub over with a coarse sandpaper, fill any cracks or holes with car-body filler, and finally work through the pack of coarse-to-smooth-graded sandpapers. If it's at all possible, do the rubbing down outdoors to avoid messing up your workshop and breathing in potentially harmful dust.

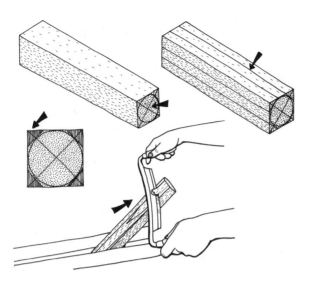

Illus. 2. Roughing out. Top left: Establish the center-point by drawing crossed diagonals. Top right: Scribe out end-circles, draw tangents to the circles, and run lines from the resultant octagon and along the length of the wood. Bottom: Use a plane, rasp, or drawknife to remove the areas of waste.

Sanding and sandpaper Sandpapers are best purchased in graded packs and used in a rough-to-smooth order. Small, difficult-to-get-at areas can be worked with the sandpaper being nailed, wrapped, or otherwise supported on a cork block and/or stick tool (Illus. 3). See **Stick tools**.

Scroll saw A power-driven, fine-bladed bench saw—sometimes called a jigsaw or fretsaw—used for cutting out sheet wood, plastic, and metal. In use, the workpiece is pushed across the worktable and fed into the blade. The blades come in many sizes and are cheap and easy to replace. The scroll saw is safe to use, as long as you hold the whole workpiece firmly down on the table, work at a steady pace, and always are ready to present the blade with the line of the next cut. The super-fast, up-and-down jigging action of the blade results in a swift, fine, accurate cut. The scroll saw is the perfect tool for working with plywood. It's espe-

cially good for cutting complex curves and enclosed windows.

Setting in The process of transferring the working drawings through to the face of the wood and making initial cuts.

Sharpening It's much easier to work with sharp tools. You need to establish the bevel on the grindstone and hone the cutting edge on the oilstone. Chisels are best sharpened with a slight rocking motion, until the full width of the bevel comes into contact with the stone and the angle has been established. Knives, on the other hand, are honed, with the blade being held down flat on the stone; stroke the blade one way and then turn the blade over for the back stroke. Try not to overheat the blade (Illus. 4).

Stick tools Variously shaped pieces of "found" wood, metal, or plastic that are used for supporting sandpaper. We use everything from lollipop sticks and old spoons to broken saw blades and pieces of

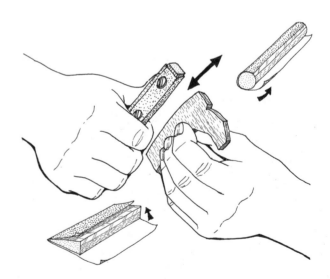

Illus. 3. Sanding. Small difficult-to-reach areas are best sanded with a stick tool. A stick is selected and covered with sandpaper, which is either nailed or attached with double-sided transparent tape. The tool is grasped and worked like a file.

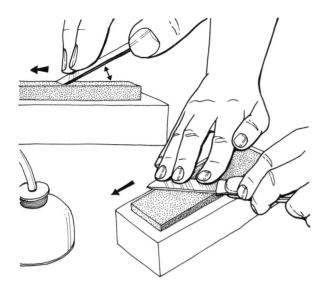

Illus. 4. Sharpening. Top left: Rock the blade from side to side, while at the same time running it along the stone. When the full width of the blade is in contact with the stone, complete the honing with long easy push strokes. Bottom: A knife blade needs to be wedge-shaped. First, stroke the blade away from you until one side is honed; then, flip the blade over and stroke in the other direction to hone the other side.

dowel. The sandpaper is wrapped around the object, held in place with nails or transparent tape, and then held and used like a file. See **Sanding and sandpaper.**

Straight saw Any straight, flat-bladed woodworking saw that does the job.

Templates A pattern, shape, or image cut out from thin sheet wood or cardboard; a shape that is drawn around and used to reproduce a number of identical shapes. In the context of wood turning, a template can be used as a profile guide. In use, the template is held up against the workpiece and then the waste is removed, until the template profile fits snugly against the wood being turned.

Tracing paper A strong transparent paper used for transferring the lines of the design from the master drawing through to the wood. When you come to trace off a design,

or pencil-press-transfer a design through to the wood, always make sure that the tracing paper is well secured with tabs of masking tape. See also **Pencils and pencil-press-transferring**.

Try square Also simply called a square. If you want to test your work for straightness or for 90° angles, then you need a square. It's best to get one with a wooden stock and a metal blade.

Turned beads A term loosely used to describe all the small delicate dips and curves that go into making up turned spindles, skittles, and doll-like forms. Using a beading or parting tool, the working action is as follows: Cut from high to low wood, pivot the tool on the rest and roll it as the cut proceeds, and then raise the handle to complete the cut.

V-block A wooden block used to support a round section of wood. Blocks can easily be tailor-made from scrap wood to suit the shape of the workpiece. In use, the workpiece is supported or cradled in the "V."

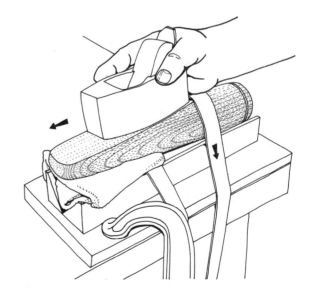

Illus. 5. V-block. A V-block used in conjunction with a foot strap makes a good clamp for holding difficult-to-grip profiles.

Used with a hold-down foot strap, a long V-block is especially good for supporting and controlling long round sections (Illus. 5).

Varnish For the projects in this book, it's best to use a clear or golden, high-gloss polyurethane varnish.

Vise A bench-mounted screw clamp, used for holding and securing wood while it is being worked.

Wheels Toymakers need wheels. There are bead-wheels and rollers, casters and glides, thin plastic wheels, fat wooden wheels, wheels made on the lathe, and wheels fretted out on the scroll saw, in all kinds of variations and sizes. Some wheels are glued on the axles, others are fitted with screws and washers, and still others are loosely fitted on stub axles. In making wooden pull-along toys, it's always a good idea to determine the type and size of the wheels right at the start of the project (Illus. 6).

Whittling From the Anglo-Saxon word *thwi-tan*, meaning to cut and pare with a small knife. In some way or other, many toys need to be whittled: Slices need to be taken from turnings, dowel-ends need to be whittled to make hands, and so on. We tend to use a craft knife, a Northwest Coast Indian crooked knife, a scalpel, and a penknife.

Workbench Regardless of whether it's a table out in the garage, an old kitchen table in a spare room, or a specially built carpenter's bench, your workbench must be strong, stable, at the correct height, clean, and fitted with a vise.

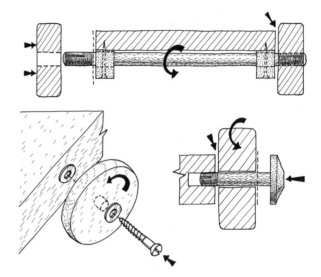

Illus. 6. Wheels. Top: Wooden wheels glued to wooden dowel axles; the axles are free-turning within the bearing blocks. Such wheels are good for medium-to-large toys. Bottom left: For small toys, the wheels can be screwed directly to the side of the base. Bottom right: Also for small toys, lathe-turned wheels can be mounted on small lathe-turned mushroom-stub axles.

Working drawing The scaled, measured, or full-size drawing, from which measurements are taken. See **Designing**.

Working face The best side of the wood, the side that shows, the side that is going to be on view once the toy has been put together.

Work-out paper Paper on which all the details are sketched and worked out prior to making the project. We use a hardcover sketchbook for all the initial designs and small details. For the full-size patterns, we use lengths of end-of-roll printer's or decorator's paper.

PROJECTS

1
A PULL-ALONG LADY
ON A HORSE

A horse on a round ball-wheel base,
with a dolly-peg equestrienne

Primary techniques: turning, fretting, whittling,
fitting, and painting

Wild West rodeo horses, medieval knights on proud chargers, beautiful acrobatic equestriennes on circus horses, fierce cossack horses, horses pulling carriages . . . of all the animals used in toys, the horse is certainly one of the most popular. There are any number of toy horses in museums that bear witness to the fact that, as far back as ancient Rome, Greece, and Egypt, and right through to modern times, the horse has held pride of place in the hearts and minds of countless generations of children.

For our pull-along horse, we drew our inspiration from two sources: folk-toy horses that were made in the seventeenth, eighteenth, and nineteenth centuries in the Erzgebirge mountains in Saxony, a region on the German and Czechoslovakian border, and folk-toy horses that were made in the nineteenth century in northeast Poland. Such toy horses are characterized by being lathe-turned, naïvely painted in bright primary colors, and set on little wheeled stands, and by having curious dolly-peg riders. The push-fit dolly-peg riders are good fun, in that they can be removed, set back to front, set on the side like circus riders, and so on.

If you enjoy working on the lathe and are looking for a small, delicate, really beautiful

Illus. 1. Project picture.

traditional toy horse to make, a toy that will put your wood-turning skills to the test, then this is the project for you.

Design and Technique Considerations

Study the working drawings (Illus. 2 and 3) and consider how, at a grid scale of four squares to 1″, the total horse and rider is about 7 to 8″ high, 6″ long from nose to tail, and 6″ wide across the base. Note, especially, the way the ball-wheels are made from large wooden beads that are set in holes and pivoted on hidden dowel-pin axles.

From a wood turner's viewpoint, the project is all the more exciting in that the body of the horse and the dolly-peg lady can be turned all of a piece from the same length of wood.

Study the details and sections, and see how the lady's proud, straight-backed, high-bosomed, broad-hipped profile has been achieved by taking the initial dolly-peg turning and slicing it away at the back and front.

Bear in mind that, apart from the three primary turnings—the horse's body, the lady, and the base disc—the other components are either shop-bought or cut with a saw and knife. For instance, the legs are made from ⅜″-diameter dowel, the horse's head is worked with a coping saw from a scrap of ¾″-thick beech, and the ball-wheels are made from 1″-diameter, plain-varnished wooden beads. With that said, if you are really keen to demonstrate your wood-turning prowess, then there's no reason why you shouldn't modify the project and go the whole hog and make everything on the lathe. You could give the horse four fancy turned spindle legs, the ball-wheels could be turned, and even the horse's head could be a quarter of a flat-turned disc—it's a thought! (See the pendulum horses, project 4.)

Tools and Materials

- A 15″ length of best-quality 2½ × 2½″-square beech—for the dolly-peg lady and the body of the horse.
- A ¾″-thick slab of beech at 6½ × 6½″—for the base.
- A ¾″-thick slab of beech at 2½ × 2½″—for the horse's head.
- A 20″ length of ⅜″ dowel—for the horse's legs.
- A 12″ length of ¼″ dowel—for the ball-wheel pivot pins.
- Four 1″-diameter, plain-varnished wooden beads—for the wheels.
- A sheet each of work-out and tracing paper.
- The use of a lathe.
- A screw chuck to fit the lathe.
- A good selection of wood-turning tools.
- A compass and a pair of dividers.
- A pencil and ruler.
- A drill press with bits at ¾″, ⅜″, and ¼″ diameter.
- A small hand drill.
- A straight saw and a coping saw.
- A pair of wooden V-blocks—they are easy to make from scrap wood.
- A craft knife.
- A ¾″-wide chisel—for the neck-mortise slot.
- A pack of graded sandpapers.
- Acrylic paints in red, green, and black.
- A can of clear varnish.
- A 5″ length of ½″-diameter rope—for the tail.
- A brass screw-eye for the pull-cord.
- A length of thin cord.
- A small amount of PVA wood glue.
- A couple of small brushes: a broad and a fine-point.
- All the usual workshop items, such as old cloths, brush cleaner, newspaper, and disposable paint cans.

Setting and Roughing Out

When you have studied the working drawings (Illus. 2 and 3) and have a clear understanding of how the toy needs to be worked and put together, set the various pieces of wood out on the workbench and check them over for faults. Bearing in mind that the wood is to be turned and that selected areas—the lady's face, the body and legs of the horse, and the base slab—are to remain unpainted, avoid wood that looks in any way to be less than

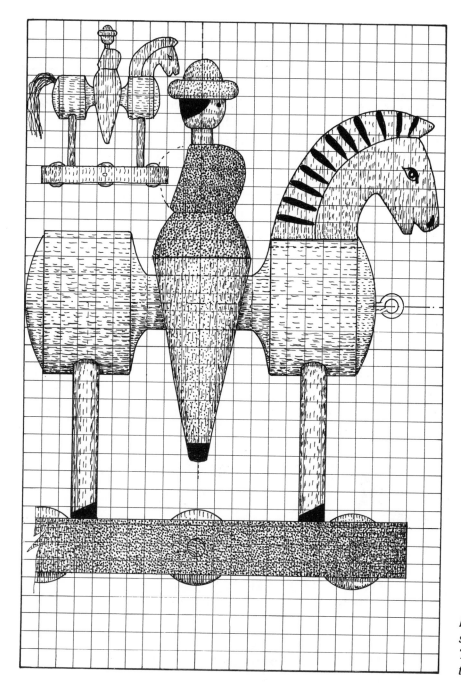

Illus. 2. Working drawing. The scale is four grid squares to 1″. The small inset (top left) is not to scale.

perfect. If, for example, there are splits, stains, or dead knots, then choose another piece.

When you are pleased that the wood is all it should be, take the 15″ length of 2½ × 2½″-square beech—or another straight-grained, easy-to-turn wood of your own choosing—and establish the end center-points by drawing crossed diagonals. Having made sure that the lathe is in good condition, mount the wood between the lathe centers and set the tool rest just a fraction below the center-point height. Before you turn on the power, run through the pre-switch checklist (see "Lathe safety" on page 17). For example, is your hair tied back, are your cuffs rolled up, are the tools close at hand but out of harm's way? All such points need to be carefully considered before you start to use what is potentially a dangerous piece of equipment. When everything is in order, switch on the power and use the round-nosed gouge to swiftly turn the wood down to a 2¼″-diameter cylinder.

Then take the skew chisel and turn the wood down to a smooth 2″-diameter cylinder.

Turning Off the Horse and Lady Profiles

When you have achieved a good smooth clean 2″-diameter cylinder, take a pencil, ruler, and dividers, and set the wood out along its length, with all the step-offs that go into making up

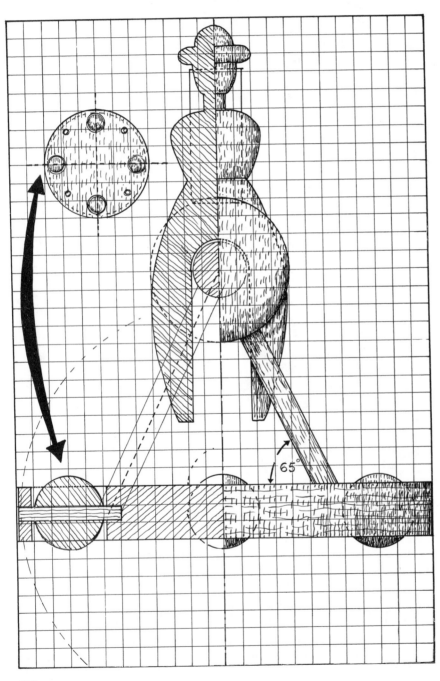

65°

Illus. 3. Working drawing. The scale is four grid squares to 1″. The small inset is not to scale.

the design (Illus. 4, top). From left to right along the length of the wood, allow 1½″ for headstock waste, ¼″ for the curve at one end of the horse's body, 1¼″ for one end of the horse, ¼″ for the saddle curve, 1½″ for the saddle, ¼″ for the other saddle curve, 1¼″ for the other end of the horse's body, ¼″ for the curve at the end of the horse, 1″ for waste, 1″ for the lady's head-hat-face area, ¼″ for her neck, 1″ for her bosom, 3½″ for the legs, and a final 1½″ for tailstock waste. Use the dividers to make positive step-off marks; score grooves into the wood to a depth of about 1/16″. When this is done, take a pencil and work along the turning, clearly marking the areas of waste that can be directly stepped and lowered. You will be able to lower the headstock waste, the flat 1½″ middle-of-saddle area (meaning the area between the curves), the waste between the horse and the lady, the lady's head-hat area, and the tailstock waste.

Having established the areas of waste that

need to be cleared, take the parting tool and sink depth guides on the waste side of the grooved step-off marks. So, for example, with the middle-of-saddle area, the two guides—one at each end—need to be sunk to a depth of ⅝″, so as to leave a central core that measures ¾″ in diameter. And at the head-hat area, the guides need to be cut in to a depth of ½″, so as to leave you with a 1″-diameter central core. When you have established the depth at various points along the turning, use the tool of your choice to clear away the bulk of the waste.

Once you have achieved the basic steps and levels that set out the design, then comes the exciting task of turning off the various curves. If you look at Illus. 2, you will see that with the horse, there are four curves in all: two convex curves, one at the front and the other at the rear, and a concave curve at each end of the saddle. Use the skew chisel to cut the convex curves and the small round-nosed gouge for the concave saddle curves. Work in the direction of the grain, that is, from high peak areas, down and in towards the valleys (Illus. 4, middle).

Continue in this manner with all the curves that make up the contours of the dolly-peg lady: the curves of the hat, face, and chin, the curve of the bosom, and the large, slow, broad curve that runs down from the waist to the feet. Mark in the bottom of the jacket with a small groove (Illus. 4, bottom).

Finally, when you have what you consider are good clean shapes, turn the wood down to a smooth finish, give the turning a swift rubdown with a fine-grade sandpaper, and then use the point of the skew chisel to part the work off from the lathe.

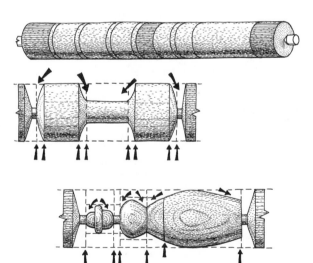

Illus. 4. Turning. Top: Set the wood out with all the step-offs that go into making up the design. Middle: The horse's body. The small arrows on the underside indicate the position of the individual step-offs; the large arrows show the direction of the cut. Bottom: The lady. The arrows on the underside show the initial step-offs; the arrows on the top show the direction of the cut.

Turning Off the Base Disc

Take the 6½ × 6½″-square, ¾″-thick slab of beech and find its center-point by drawing two crossed diagonals. Set the compass to a radius of 3″, spike the point on the center-point, and scribe out a 6″-diameter circle (Illus. 5, top

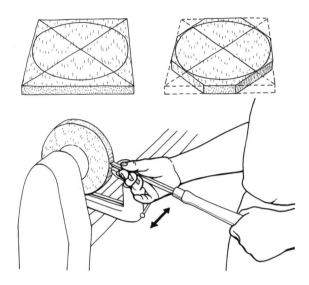

Illus. 5. Top left: Find the center of the wood by drawing crossed diagonals; scribe out a 6"-diameter circle. Top right: Draw tangents at the four diagonal intersections of the circle, and use a straight or flat saw to cut away the bulk of the waste. Bottom: Turn the octagonal slab down to a smooth-edged 6"-diameter disc.

left). Draw tangents at the four diagonal intersections of the circle, and use the straight saw to cut away the resultant corners of waste (Illus. 5, top right). Mount the screw chuck on the headstock, and screw the board in position on the lathe. With the board secure and nicely centered, bring the tool rest around to the side of the lathe bed so that you can approach the workpiece edge on. Having gone through your pre-switch-on checklist, switch on the power and use the tool(s) of your choice to turn the octagonal slab down to a smooth-edged 6"-diameter disc (Illus. 5, bottom). Now rub the edges down to a good finish and remove the workpiece from the lathe.

Shaping the Dolly-Peg Lady

First take a look at Illus. 3 and Illus. 6, top left, and see how the shape has been achieved by slicing and sawing the turning. The initial slicing is straightforward enough. With the turning in one hand, a knife in the other, and

looking at the figure in side-view profile, mark the turning "back" and "front." Then swiftly slice away the wood between the waist and the neck to make the lady's back (see project 4, Illus. 8) and from the hips, "back" and "front," to the feet to give the lady her stylized legs. Don't attempt any realistic curves; simply cut away flat smooth plains, so as to leave the wood looking crisp and level.

When you have achieved the flat plains at the back and front of the figure, set the turning feet up in the jaws of a rag-muffled vise and start to work with the straight saw and the coping saw, clearing away the between-leg waste. Again, don't try for any fancy shapes; merely run two straight saw cuts down into the turning that are just under ¾" apart and 2" long (Illus. 6, top center). Then take the coping saw and link the two cuts with a smooth ¾"-diameter half-circle curve (Illus. 6, top right). If all goes well, the waste should fall

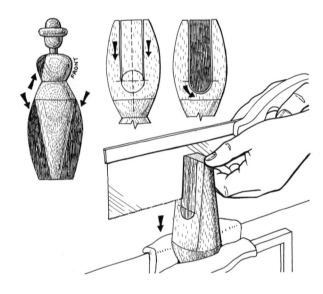

Illus. 6. Top left: Slice away the waste in the direction of the arrows, removing all the shaded areas. Top center and bottom right: With a straight saw, cut on the waste side of the drawn line, making two 2"-long cuts just under ¾" apart. Top right: Use the coping saw to link the two cuts with a smooth ¾"-diameter half-circle curve, making sure that the cut is on the waste side of the drawn line.

away, leaving a bridgelike form that is a tight peglike fit on the horse. If you are at all worried about cutting away too much wood, it's best to err on the cautious side and cut away a small amount of waste and then whittle to a good fit.

Now take a piece of sandpaper and rub the cut faces down to a smooth finish.

Cutting the Horse's Head

Trace the horse's head off to size, and carefully pencil-press-transfer the traced profile through to the small piece of ¾"-thick pine. Don't forget to allow an extra ¼" for the body-to-neck mortise joint, where the neck shape in side view swells to match the end-body profile. Make sure that the grain of the wood runs from the top to the bottom, that is, from the top of the mane, down through to the base of the neck (Illus. 2). When this is done, set the wood in the vise and use the coping saw to fret out the profile. Using the coping saw is easy enough, as long as you follow three simple rules: The saw blade must be well tensioned, the line of cut should run a little to the waste side of the drawn line, and the blade should run through the thickness of the wood so that the sawn edge/face is at right angles to the working face.

When you have achieved a crisp, clean-edged profile, use the graded sandpapers to rub the head down to a smooth, slightly round-edged finish. Leave the base of the neck squarely cut and sharp-edged.

Cutting the Head Slot and the Leg Holes

Look back at Illus. 2 and see how the head is slotted into a body mortise. Note that the head mortise is ¾" wide, 1¼" long, and ¼" deep. See how, at the end view of the section, the head is set on the center-line at top-center, or 0°. Draw in a center-line from 0° through to 180°, and then mark in the position of the head

mortise in relationship to the line (Illus. 7, top left). When you come to cutting the mortise slot, first establish the width of the mortise by making two ¼"-deep saw cuts, being sure that the cuts are ¾" apart and on the waste side of the drawn line. Then use the ¾"-wide chisel to clear the waste away to the depth of the cuts (Illus. 7, top right). Aim for a mortise slot that is a tight push-fit for the head.

Look back at Illus. 3, left side, and note how, in cross section, the legs occur at 25° at either side of the bottom-center, or at the 180° mark, whereas in side view, the legs look to be vertical and are set on a center-line that divides the 1¼" length of each half-body.

Measure ⅝" along from both the head and tail ends, and draw in center-lines that run right around the body girth. With the turning secured upside down on a V-block, locate the

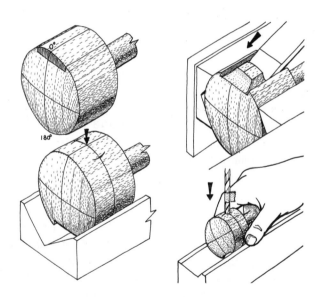

Illus. 7. Top left: Draw in and center the position of the head mortise. Top right: Secure the workpiece between V-blocks, and use the ¾"-wide chisel to clear the waste away to the depth of the cuts. Bottom left: Locate the position of the leg holes by setting a compass to a radius of ½" and scribing arcs that intersect the center-line. Bottom right: Use the drill press to sink a ⅜"-diameter hole. The little tab of tape ½" up from the point acts as a depth gauge.

31

position of the leg holes by setting the compass to a radius of ½", spiking the point on the 180° bottom-center mark, and scribing arcs that intersect the center-line (Illus. 7, bottom left). Do this at both ends of the horse. Make sure that each of the four hole-centers is clearly marked. Now, one hole at a time and with the workpiece still supported on the V-block, slowly rotate the turning until the hole-center is uppermost and then use the drill press to sink a ⅜"-diameter hole down into the wood to a depth of ½" (Illus. 7, bottom right).

When you have made the four leg holes, cut the ⅜" dowel into 5" lengths and have a trial dry-run fitting.

Fitting the Ball-Wheels

Once you have made the horse's head, body, and legs, the dolly-peg lady, and the base disc, then comes the exciting, if not tricky, task of fitting the ball-wheels.

Take the 6"-diameter base disc and rub out the initial diagonal work-out lines. With pencil, ruler, and square, redraw the crossed center-lines so that they are set at right angles to each other and they run both with and across the grain of the wood. Locate the center of the ball-wheel holes by measuring from the edge of the disc and ¾" along each of the four radius lines (Illus. 8, top). When you have clearly located the center of the ball-wheel holes, set the 1⅛" spade or flat bit in the drill press, support the workpiece on a sheet of waste wood, and bore the holes through. Take a pencil and, with the grain running from front to back, label the four holes "front," "back," "left," and "right." Now, in relationship to the rotation of the ball-wheels and the resultant position of the dowel-pin axle, use a pencil and ruler to draw in each of the axle center-lines. There's no problem when it comes to the two side wheels; the axle line simply runs in from the side of the disc and cuts across the hole. But it's not so easy with the "front" and "back" wheels. As the axles need to be set at right

angles to the front-to-back center-line and parallel to the side-wheel axles, so the "front" and "back" axle lines have to run 1⅜" across the face of the disc before they even start to cut across the hole. You will have to drill in from both sides of the wheel hole. Draw in the axle lines and run them straight on down the ¾"-edge thickness.

When you have fixed the position, angle, and run of the four axle lines, secure the disc in the jaws of the vise, set a length of ¾" waste dowel in the hole to stop drill-exit splitting, set the ¼"-diameter bit in the hand drill, and bore out the holes (Illus. 8, bottom). Although there is no easy way of ensuring that the axle holes will be true, you won't go far wrong as long as you set the point of the drill bit halfway down the ¾" slab thickness and make sure

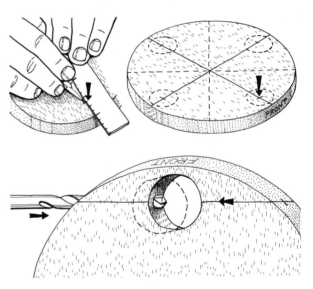

Illus. 8. Top: Locate the centers of the ball-wheel holes by measuring from the edge of the disc and ¾" along the radius lines. Bottom: Secure the disc in the vise, place a waste dowel in the wheel hole, follow the guidelines, and run holes in from each side.

that the drill is aligned with the pencil-drawn axle lines.

Having drilled out the axle holes, simply rub the ¼"-diameter dowels down slightly so that they are an easy fit, locate the wooden beads

This pull-along Noah's Ark toy, painted with traditional imagery, is project 7, page 81.

Painted with traditional fairground imagery, this swinging-pendulum toy is project 4, page 53.

B

The "old woman who lived in a shoe" toy is project 13, page 131.

Top: The duck, project 3, page 43, has cam-operated up-and-down "swimming" movement. Bottom: The ladybug, project 14, page 140, has a friction-drive cradled-ball body.

This 1918 biplane, project 10, page 107, has a flick-around propeller.

D

in the holes, cut the dowel-pins to length, and groove the ends. The wheel-pins are glued at a later stage.

Fitting the Head and Legs

Fitting the horse's head is pretty straightforward; all you do is smear glue on mating surfaces—in the mortise slot and on the bottom edge of the head—and then slide the head into position (Illus. 9, left). The same goes for fitting the dowel legs into the body of the horse. You just cut slots along the end of the dowel, smear a small amount of glue over mating surfaces, and then slide or tap the legs into the holes.

When you come to fitting the horse's legs into the base, take a look at Illus. 2 and 3 and see how the legs are angled so that they strike the base at a 65° angle and are set so that there is a vertical distance between the under-

side of the horse and the base of 2″. See, also, how the horse is positioned on the base so that it is aligned with the "front" and the "front" center-line, and is centered with the disc.

Start by cutting the legs down so that they are 2¾″ long, which allows 2⅜″ for the leg length and ⅜″ for the into-base attachment. With pencil, ruler, and compass, carefully locate the position of the legs in relationship to the wheel holes and the center-lines. If all is correct, in end view, the hoof center-points should be 3″ apart and strike the base 1½″ out from the front-to-back center-line, whereas, in side view, the feet or hooves should be 3¼″ apart and strike the base 1⅝″ out from the side-to-side center-line. Draw all the guidelines out on the face of the disc, and positively fix the dowel-center position of the four feet.

Having fixed the position of the legs, cut a piece of waste so that it is angled at 65°, clamp a scrap of wood to the base to act as a stop for the jig, set the ⅜″-diameter bit in the hand drill, and use the angled jig to bore out the four foot holes (Illus. 9, right). Sink the holes to an angled depth of between ⅜ and ½″. When you have made the four holes, cut glue slots on the bottom ⅜″ of the legs, smear glue on mating surfaces, and slide the feet into their holes. You might need to tap the body with a block and hammer to achieve correct alignment. While the drill is in hand, bore out the ½″-diameter tail hole. Place the wheels, run the dowels through the holes, and fasten with glue. Finally, when the glue is dry, rub the dowel ends down flush with the edge of the base disc.

Painting and Finishing

Turn back to the project picture (Illus. 1) and the working drawing (Illus. 2), and see how the various parts are either left plain or painted. The body of the horse, the horse's legs, and the ball-wheels are left plain, whereas the base and the lady's coat are painted bright red, the lady's hat and trousers

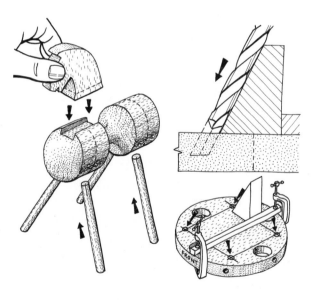

Illus. 9. Left: Glue the horse's head in the mortise slot. For the leg's, cut slots along the end of the dowels, put a small amount of glue on the end of the dowels and in the holes, and tap them into the holes. Right: Positively fix the dowel-center position of the four feet. Cut a piece of waste so that it is angled at 65°, and use it when you come to bore out the leg holes to set the angle of the drill.

are painted green, and all the details of the faces, feet, buttons, hair, and mane are brought out in black.

Move the horse and rider to the dust-free area that you have set aside for painting, set out all your acrylic paints and the brushes, spread newspaper over the work surface, and generally get ready for painting. With the main areas of paint being brushed on as flat color, it's a fairly straightforward process. The base is painted bright red, the hat green, and so forth. When you come to painting the details that make up the horse's mane, all you do is load the small brush with paint and then repeatedly set down the loaded brush so as to "print" the characteristic teardrop form. A line of such daubs set around the top curve on both sides of the horse's head makes for an exciting pattern detail. And so you continue painting the details—the horse's eyes, the dots for the lady's eyes, and so on—until the toy is well accentuated in black.

When the paint is dry, give the whole toy a couple of coats of clear varnish and put it to one side to dry. Finally, when the varnish is dry, glue the rope into the tail hole, screw the large screw-eye into the front of the base, tie on the pull-cord, and . . . the dolly-peg lady is ready for her first canter around the hills and dales of the playroom.

Hints and Modifications

- If you like the overall idea of the toy but want to create more complex imagery, you could shape the legs of the horse, whittle and taper the top edge of the horse's mane, pattern the saddle, pattern the edge of the base disc, and so on.
- The turnings need to be free from knots and splits, so spend time choosing your wood. Select a strong easy-to-turn wood like beech, ash, or American cherry.
- If you do decide to use an exotic wood, make sure that it is tight-grained, splinter-proof, and completely nontoxic. If you have doubts, contact a specialist supplier.
- The dolly-peg lady needs to be a tight push-fit on the horse. So make sure, when you are making the two straight-down cuts for the legs, that they are parallel to each other and no more than ¾" apart. To this end, make sure that the cuts are to the waste side of the drawn line.
- If you prefer plain-wood toys, you could detail the features with a pyrography tool and give the entire workpiece a couple of coats of clear varnish (see project 2).
- You could have a square base and use ordinary wheels instead of the ball-wheels that are more difficult to fit.

2
A PULL-ALONG CRANDALL COW

A flat-wood cow with a pivotal head, neck, and tail

Primary techniques: scroll-sawing, pyrography drawing, drilling, and assembling

Crandall-type flat figures take their name from a certain Crandall family who lived and worked in and around Pennsylvania from about the early 1830s onwards. Crandall figures are characterized by being made from flat plywood, by having riveted, pinned, or pivotal joints, and by being presented on a grooved stand or base. The idea is, that once the arms and legs have been moved around on their pivots, the figures can be set upright and slotted in the grooved base.

Our Crandall-type cow-and-calf toy is special, in that not only does the head pivot on the neck, do the neck and tail pivot within the body, and do both the cow and calf fit into a slotted, or grooved, base, but the whole arrangement has been set on wheels. Another unusual feature is that the design details of the cow and calf are drawn onto the surface of the unpainted wood with a pyrography pen.

Design and Technique Considerations

Study Illus. 6 and see how, at a scale of four grid squares to 1″, the cow is about 6″ long and 4″ high. Note the way the head pivots on the neck, and the neck and tail in the body, so as to produce a very realistic movement. Now take a look at Illus. 2 and see how, at a scale of two grid squares to 1″, the grooved stand is about 7″ long and 4½″ wide across the span of the wheels. Note the use of ¼″-thick plywood throughout—for the layers that make up the cow and the calf, and for the base slab.

Consider the way wooden dowels are used so that they can only be seen, on the cow's head, as dowel ends. With the design features being burnt into the plywood with a pyrography tool, and the plywood being matt-varnished and waxed, the friction between the layers of wood is enough to hold the cow in

Illus. 1. Project picture.

its set position. The absence of washers between the plywood layers makes for an easy ¼" spacing of the ¼ × ¼"-square strips that make up the grooved base. The five-layer cow and the single-layer calf can be arranged anywhere on the base. For maximum child-play safety, the ¼" base strips have been glued as well as nailed. The glue cancels out the potential danger of the nails.

The feet have ¼"-long additions so that when the figures are slotted into the base grooves, the details of the feet stay visible. Also, note how the project uses shop-bought wheels and axles, with the axles being held in position by two screwed skidlike axle bearing blocks.

Tools and Materials

- A sheet of ¼"-thick best-quality white-faced multicore plywood at 10 × 7"—for the animals.
- A sheet of ¼"-thick best-quality white-faced multicore plywood at 7 × 3¾"—for the base slab.
- A 60" length of prepared ¼ × ¼"-square wood—for the beading on the base (this allows a good amount for wastage).
- A 15" length of prepared ½ × ½"-square white pine—for the two long axle blocks.
- A 6" length of ¼" hardwood dowel—for the pivots.
- The use of a scroll saw—we use a Hegner.
- A piece each of work-out and tracing paper.
- A pencil, a ruler, and dividers.
- A bradawl.
- A drill press with a ¼"-diameter drill bit.
- A small sharp craft knife.
- A pack of graded sandpapers and a cork block.
- An electric pyrography tool.
- A pair of soft leather work gloves—to use with the pyrography tool.
- A work board.
- A small amount of white PVA wood glue.
- A small amount of Super Glue.

- A pair of small C-clamps.
- A hammer and a nail punch.
- A can of clear, matt, sheen varnish.
- A medium-fine paint brush.
- A small amount of wax furniture polish.
- All the usual workshops items, such as brass screws, brads, brush cleaner, old cloths, and newspaper.

Cutting, Drilling, and Shaping

When you have a good clear understanding of how the toy needs to be made and put together, draw the design up to size and set out all your tools and materials so that they are conveniently close at hand. Take a tracing of all the parts that go into making up the cow and the calf (Illus. 3), and then, with the tracing paper held secure with tabs of masking tape, carefully pencil-press-transfer the traced profiles through to the best face of the 9 × 6" sheet of ¼"-thick plywood (Illus. 4, top). When the transferred images look crisp and clear (you might need to rework any indistinct lines), remove the tracing and label the various drawn forms "cow's front-left leg," "cow's left cheek," and so on.

Double-check the position of all the dowel/pivot holes and then mark the hole-centers with a bradawl (Illus. 4, bottom). Set the ¼" bit in the drill, support the workpiece on a piece of scrap wood, and carefully bore each hole through. Make sure that the holes run at right angles to the working face of the plywood. Having checked that the scroll saw is in good condition and that the blade is correctly set and tensioned, switch on the power and set to work, cutting out the various profiles. If you are a beginner with the scroll saw, it's best to have a preproject tryout with a few scraps of wood. Experiment with blade sizes, blade tension, and angles of approach, until you are able to work with ease and confidence. It's all pretty straightforward, as long as you hold the wood down firmly on the saw table, work at a steady even pace, and are always ready to smoothly present the blade with the line of the next cut. Aim, when you are cutting, to work a little to the waste side of the drawn line. It's a good idea to first cut the plywood into manageable shapes and then to cut each shape out with short controlled "bites" (Illus. 5, top).

When you have made the 13 cutouts that compose the design—the four cow's legs, the two body sides, the central body and neck, the central body udders, the three pieces that make up the head, the tail, and the little calf—rub all the holes and sawn edges down with the graded sandpapers until all surfaces are smooth to the touch.

Identify the two side-view head cutouts, and

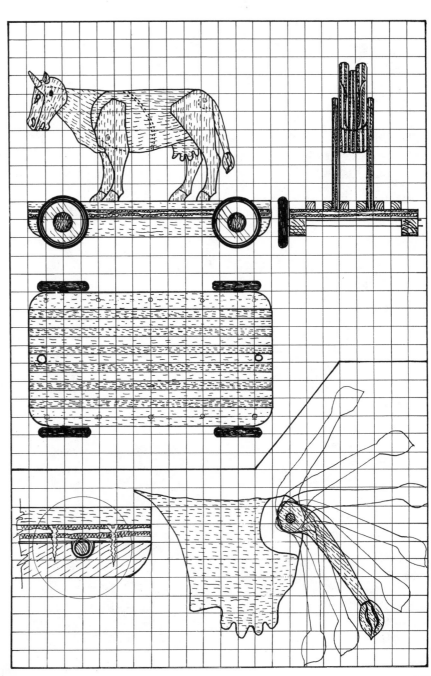

Illus. 2. Working drawing. The scale is four grid squares to 1". Note the section details, the plan of the base, the attachment of the axle blocks, and the tail movement.

then take the knife and swiftly slice off the two small areas of waste at both sides (Illus. 5, bottom). Finally, make a tracing of the pyrography details—the horns, ears, eyes, nostrils, mouth, hooves, and tail—and transfer these designs through to the cutouts. Don't forget that the details are burnt onto both faces of the wood.

Drawing In the Design and Putting the Parts Together

Having drawn in the lines that make up the details of the design, switch on the pyrography tool and allow the point to heat to a dull-red glow. Wearing a leather glove on the hand

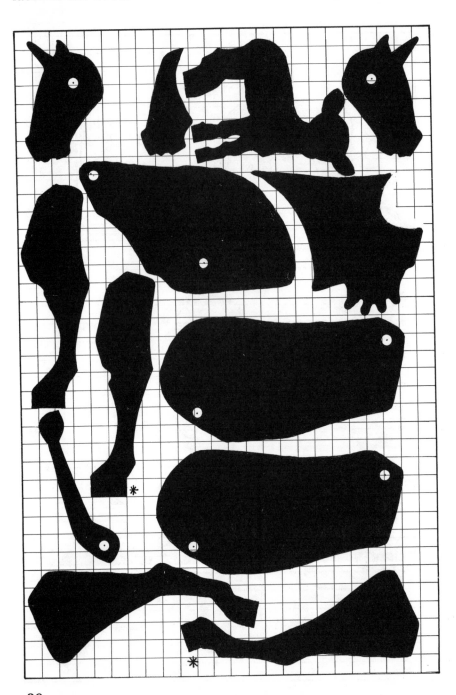

Illus. 3. Diagrammatic cutting grid. The scale is four grid squares to 1". The asterisks indicate the front and back legs for one side—the legs as seen on the far side in Illus. 2, top.

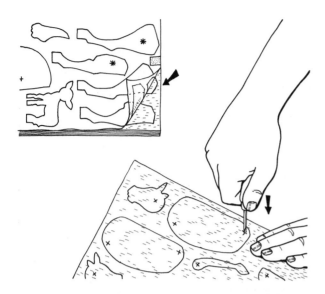

Illus. 4. Top: With the tracing paper held securely with tabs of masking tape, transfer the traced lines through to the best face of the plywood. Bottom: Use a bradawl to mark in the centers of the dowel holes.

that's holding the wood and working on a work board (just in case you slip), run through a test on a scrap of wood. A slow stroke will produce a dark heavy line, whereas short quick strokes will produce more delicate lines. When you have mastered the tool, very carefully burn the lines of the design into the face of the wood. Drag rather than push the tool, trying to achieve a burnt line that is smooth and positive (Illus. 7, top). Be careful not to press too hard, go too deep, or blur the outline. When you have what you consider to be crisp images, give the neck piece and the tail a thin coat of varnish and hang them up on wire hooks to dry.

Take the three layers that make up the head and the three layers that make up the body, and set them out in their correct three-layer order (Illus. 7, bottom). If necessary, trim and adjust the edges for a good fit. When you are happy with the arrangement, smear PVA glue on all mating surfaces and clamp up. Be sure to use pieces of scrap wood between the clamps and the workpiece so as not to damage the face of the wood.

When the varnish on the neck and the tail units is dry, give them a generous polishing with wax. Concentrate your efforts on the parts that are to be set within the body slots. The idea is that not only will the wax make for easy movement of the parts within their slots, but it will also resist the glue when you come to fitting the dowel pivots. A piece at a time, fit the top end of the neck into the head slot, the base of the neck into the body slot, and the tail into the body slot, and pivot them in place with lengths of dowel. Adjust the friction-fit between the moving parts by squeezing the sides together with the clamps; then mark the dowels to size and cut them to length. When you are happy with the movement and fit, run

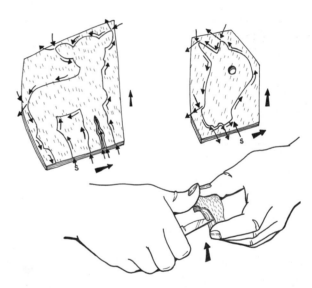

Illus. 5. Top: Cut the plywood into manageable pieces; then saw out the profiles. Work in a counterclockwise direction, starting at the "S," and clear the waste by making "bites." Bottom: Take the knife and slice away the waste at either side of the two "head" cutouts.

the dowels through the holes and glue the ends of the dowels with a small amount of Super Glue. Using a block and sandpaper, rub the ends of the dowels back so that they are flush with the surface of the plywood (Illus.

39

8, top). Then glue the legs in position on the body with Super Glue (Illus. 8, bottom). Look back at Illus. 3 and see how the legs are slightly different from one side of the cow to the other. The legs marked with an asterisk denote front and back legs for one side.

Give the workpiece a couple of coats of varnish, rubbing down between coats, but be careful not to daub areas that need to move. It's always a good idea, prior to varnishing, to prepare your work area. For example, the cow and calf could be suspended by hooks from a drying line or stood on pins or whatever. Now, take a couple of scraps of ¼" plywood, which will be used at a later stage for spacing, and give them a generous varnishing.

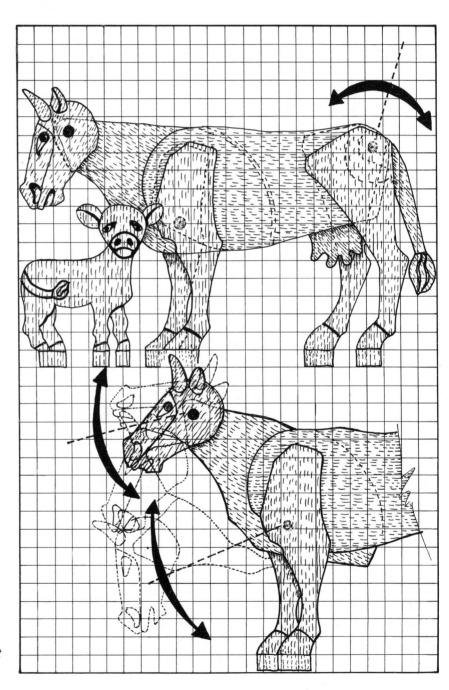

Illus. 6. Pyrography design details. The scale is four grid squares to 1". Note, also, the pivot points and the movement of the head, neck, and tail.

40

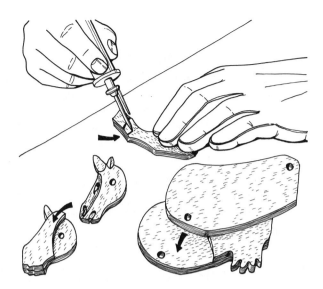

Illus. 7. Top: When the pyrography pen is at a dull-red heat, make smooth precise strokes to create positive lines. It's best to wear a leather glove to protect the hand that's holding the workpiece. Bottom: Take the three layers that make up the head and the body, and place them together in correct order.

Making the Base and Fitting the Wheels

Look back at the working-drawing details (Illus. 2), and see how the base sheet is 3¾″ wide and 7″ long, with rounded ½″-radius curves at the corners. Use a pencil, ruler, compass, and measure to set out the plywood. When everything is correct, cut the profile out on the scroll saw and bore out the two ¼″-diameter push-cord holes.

Now take the two lengths of ½ × ½″-square wood, and draw out the curve-ended skid profile for the axle bearing blocks. Each skid block needs to be 7″ long, with ½″-radius curves on both the underside and outside end-faces. Cut the curved ends on the scroll saw and rub the cut faces down to a smooth finish. Having established on each skid the base-to-block mating face, measure an inch along from the end of the block and mark in the position of the axle center-line.

Carefully relating to the diameter of your chosen shop-bought axle rods, use the scroll saw to cut out the little U-section scoops that go into making the axle bearings. Aim for a nicely contained, easy-turning fit.

Finally, countersink brass screws down through the base and screw the axle blocks into position (Illus. 2, bottom left).

Note: If the wheels are designed to turn on the axles, rather than the axles turning in the bearings, cut the U-scoops so that they are a tight-grip fit.

Making the Grooves and Finishing

Look once more at Illus. 2, and see how the base slab needs to be set out with the ¼ × ¼″-square beadings, so that the resultant ¼″-wide slots run from end to end of the slab, and the slot-and-beading sequence across the width of the base starts and finishes with a beading. Cut the six beadings to length, and rub the cut ends down with the graded sand-

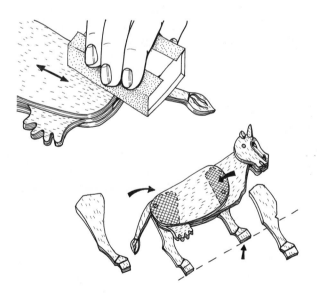

Illus. 8. Top: Use a block and sandpaper to rub the dowel ends down flush with the surface of the plywood. Bottom: Glue the legs onto the sides of the body, making sure that they are correctly paired and that the feet are level.

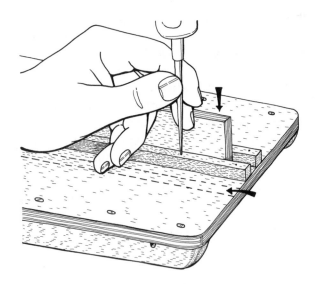

Illus. 9. Use scraps of plywood as spacers, and glue and nail the beading onto the base, working from center to side. Sink the nail heads below the surface of the wood.

papers. Using scraps of varnished ¼"-wide plywood as spacers, glue and nail the beadings in place on the top face of the base (Illus. 9). Aim for an easy push-fit of the plywood in the slots—not so tight that it is difficult for a child to set the figures in position nor so loose that they fall over. Start from the center of the base and work out towards the sides. When the glue is dry, give the base a swift rubbing down. When you have achieved a smooth finish, wipe away the dust and give the base a couple of thin coats of matt sheen varnish. Be careful not to build up a thickness between the slots.

Finally, give the whole toy a good wax polishing, slide the axles into position, fit the wheels, tie on the pull-cord, stand the cow and the calf in position on the base, and the toy is complete. *Moo....*

Hints and Modifications

- If you decide to double the scale and make a larger toy, then double the thickness of the wood and use ½"-thick plywood.
- If you like the idea of the toy but are not so happy about using dowels as pivots, then consider using such attachments as pop rivets, tap rivets, or nuts and bolts.
- Building and varnishing the base can be a bit tricky. When you are spacing the groove beadings, allow for some built-up thickness of the varnish.
- How about a ribbon and a little brass bell for the cow's neck?

3

A PULL-ALONG SWIMMING DUCK

A duck with cam-operated, up-and-down "swimming" movement

Primary techniques: fretting, turning, carving, whittling, pegging, gluing, and painting

I love ducks! When I was a kid, way back in the 1950s, I was something of a duckophile. At home, there were chalk ducks on the over-mantel, three high-relief ducks flying up the hall wall, a clutch of yellow, plastic, squeaky toy ducks in the bath—even the soap was duck-shaped. There were duck-shaped sweets, duck pictures on nursery furniture—there were ducks everywhere! And, of course, as you might expect, my toy cupboard was chock full of toy ducks. I had a sit-on rocking duck, a rubber duck with a long bendable neck and bendable legs—I even had a sweatshirt with a huge duck motif on the front and back.

But, as I recall, my favorite duck toy was a curious little prewar wooden pull-along duck that I called Yuk Duck. Made of thin plywood, Yukky was mounted on a wheeled base and fitted with a cam. As he was pulled along, he looked to be waddling slowly up and down. Yuk Duck was a really great toy—I wonder where he is now.

Design and Technique Considerations

Look at the project picture (Illus. 1) and the working drawings (Illus. 2), and see how this project can be broken down into three main

Illus. 1. Project picture.

areas: making the duck, making the base, or chassis, and turning the wheels. Now look at the diagramatic cutting grid (Illus. 3), and note how the design is beautifully simple and direct, in that the "waves" and the axle bearings are cut all of a piece from the same ply-

43

wood profile. Then study the working drawings and consider how you need four side plates in all—two of each size. See how the wave axle plates are fitted and attached—two on each side of the chassis—so as to make a pivotal support for the duck and bearings for the axles. The movement that sets the duck in motion is equally direct. The egg-shaped cam is set and attached on the axle in such a way that as it revolves, it gently tips the duck up and down (Illus. 4).

The duck itself is perhaps slightly tricky to make, but only in that it involves a small amount of carving and whittling. Study Illus. 5 and see how the duck is made in two parts. The head is roughed out, set into a body mor-

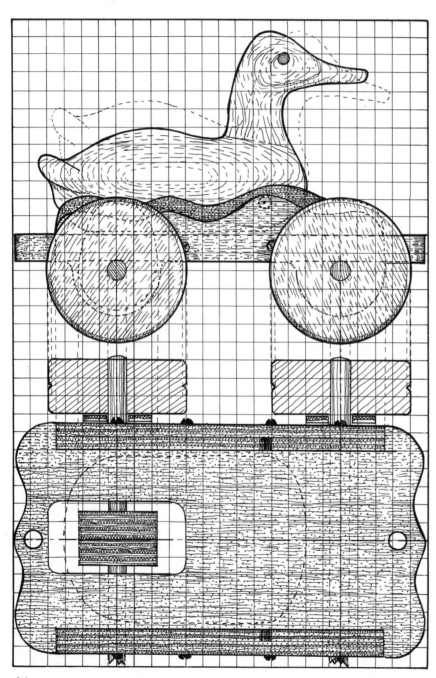

Illus. 2. Working drawings— assembly details and painting grid. The scale is approximately three grid squares to 1".

tise, glued, and dowelled, all before being whittled, sanded, and painted.

With a project involving so many techniques as this one, it's always worth considering how you might modify the techniques to suit your own needs. For example, if you enjoy whittling and scroll-saw work but are not so wild about wood turning, there's no reason why you couldn't use ready-made plastic wheels and dispense with the wood turning. On the other hand, if you like wood turning and scroll-saw work, but would rather give the whittling and carving a miss, you could build the duck from multilayered plywood and go for a scroll-sawn–slab profile. Such points need to be well considered.

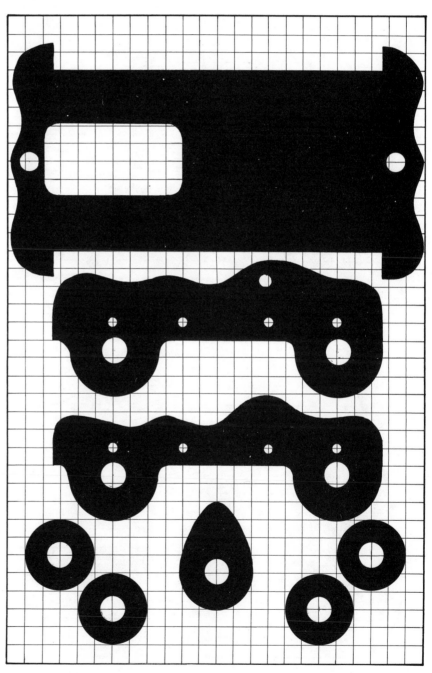

Illus. 3. Diagrammatic cutting grid. The scale is approximately three grid squares to 1".

Tools and Materials

- A sheet of best-quality ½″-thick multicore plywood that is 12″ long and 5″ wide—for the chassis base and the cam.
- A sheet of best-quality ¼″-thick multicore plywood that is 12″ long and 7″ wide—for the washers, side plates, and cam.
- A piece of 2″-thick pine that is 9″ long and 3″ wide—for the duck.
- A 10″ length of prepared 3 × 3″-square beech—for the wheels (this allows for waste).
- A 36″ length of ⅜″ dowel—for the axles, through-duck pivot, and attachment pegs.
- A 1″ length of ¼″ dowel—for the eyes.

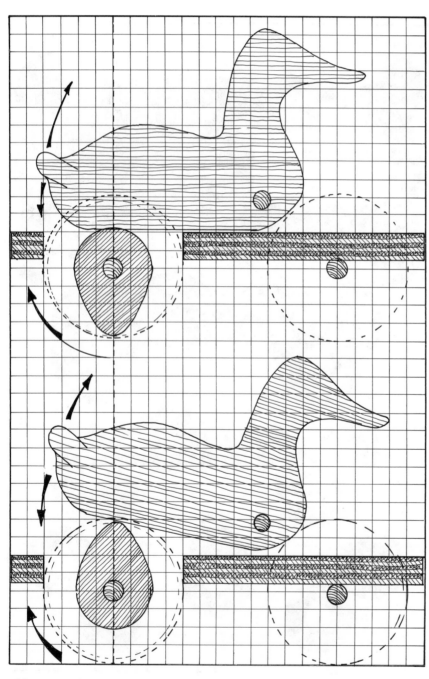

Illus. 4. Working drawings—cam movement. The scale is approximately four grid squares to 1″.

46

- The use of an electric scroll saw—we use a Hegner.
- The use of a lathe.
- A four-jaw chuck with a 3″ grip.
- A selection of turning tools.
- A 1″-mortise chisel.
- A hand drill with bits at ⅜″ and ¼″ to fit.
- A flat rasp and a tube rasp.
- A sharp knife—for whittling.
- A selection of acrylic paints.
- All the usual workshop items, such as brushes, sandpaper, paint cans, glue, varnish, screws, and screwdrivers.

Setting Out and Making the Duck

When you have a clear picture in your mind's eye of how the project needs to be worked and put together, set out all your wood and check it over for possible problems. If the wood is generally free from splits, knots, twists, and stains, label the various pieces and put them to one side in readiness.

Take the 9″-long slab of pine—the piece for the duck—and cut it into two lengths, one at 6″ and the other at 3″; then mark in crossed diagonals and a center-line on each piece. Having drawn out the body and head profiles, take clear tracings and pencil-press-transfer the traced profiles through to the working face of the wood. Take the wood a piece at a time and use the scroll saw to swiftly cut out the two profiles. Take the round-ended, boat-shaped body piece and label it "top," "front," and "side" (Illus. 6, top).

Set the body piece in the jaws of the vise, and use the rasp to cut away the sharp edges at the top and bottom. Aim for a nicely rounded form. Work one side, then another, all the while comparing the various views with each other and against Illus. 5. When you are happy with the overall body shape, use the knife and the tube rasp to carve the little ridged detail that makes up the tail. Don't aim for naturalistic realism; it's much better to go for a stylized roundness (Illus. 6, middle and bottom). When you consider the body nicely

rounded and shaped, set the workpiece topside up in the vise and cut the 1¾″-inch long, 1″-wide, ⅜″-deep neck-to-body mortise. Take the head profile and reduce the thickness until the neck comes to a good tight fit in the body mortise. When this is done, use the knife to swiftly whittle the duck's head to a stylized finish (Illus. 7, top right). Again, don't aim for detailed realism but rather try to achieve a stylized interpretation of the characteristic duck forms: the flat wide bill, the full cheeks, and the head that narrows at the top.

Having achieved a good fit with the head and body, and a convincing head shape, spread glue on mating surfaces and set the head in position in the body mortise. When the glue is dry, take the drill and the ⅜″-diameter bit and run a hole straight down through the top of the duck's head, through the neck, and into the body. Run a glued dowel down through the hole. While the drill is to hand, bore out ¼″-diameter holes for the eyes and plug them with hardwood dowels that have been stained a contrasting brown.

When you come to fitting the through-body pivotal dowel, make sure that the duck is held securely and check to see that the through-body hole is perfectly aligned with both the head-to-tail center-line and the base line (Illus. 7, bottom). To this end, pinpoint the precise position of the hole and make sure, when you are drilling, that the bit runs through the duck squarely and at right angles to the side face. It's best to enter a small-diameter pilot hole from each side of the duck and then to follow up with a ⅜″-diameter hole that runs straight through. When you are happy with the duck, take the graded sandpapers and rub all surfaces down to a silky, smooth-grained finish.

Making the Chassis Base Board

Look back at Illus. 2 and see how the chassis is made up from two thicknesses of multicore plywood: ½″ thick for the base and the drive cam, and ¼″ thick for the four side plates and the four washers. Note, also, that the cam is made up of two ½″ thicknesses.

Starting with the ½″-thick base board, first set out a center-line and then very carefully transfer all the forms and measurements through to the wood. Bear in mind, as you are setting out the design, that although many of the shapes are flexible and can be modified, certain details have to relate carefully with each other. For example, it's important that the cam hole be centered on both the center-line and the line of the axle. And the depth of the side recesses needs to relate to the two thicknesses of plywood that make up the side plates, so, if you use a different thickness of plywood, then you need to adjust the recesses

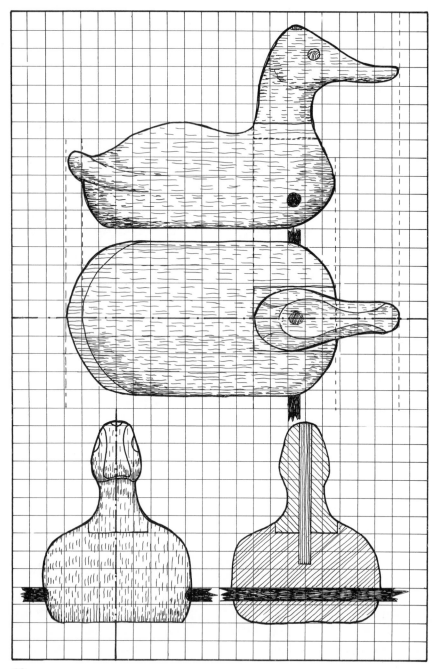

Illus. 5. Working drawings. The scale is approximately three grid squares to 1″.

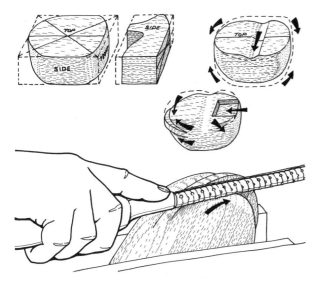

Illus. 6. Top left: Trace off the design on the two pieces of wood, and use the scroll saw to cut out the two profiles. Label the sides. Top right: Use the file to create a rounded body. Middle: Cut and file away the waste wood from the tail, and cut the 1¾″-long, 1″-wide, ⅜″-deep neck-mortise slot. Bottom: Hold the work secure in a vise, and run the file from outside to center, working above and below the "tail" on both sides.

accordingly. The cam hole is 2½″ long and 1½″ wide and centered with the center-line and the axle. The axles have to be aligned with each other and set 1½″ along from the front of the base and 2″ along from the back. Spend time getting it just right.

Having double-checked to make sure that all is correct, move the workpiece to the scroll saw and very carefully cut out the rather complicated profiles. There are two main points to remember as you are sawing: The line of cut should be on the waste side of the drawn line, and the saw blade must be running through the wood at right angles to the working face. If you follow these two rules of thumb, you won't go far wrong. When you come to cutting out the cam hole, first drill out the corners with, say, a ⅜″-diameter drill and then use one of the holes as an entry point for the scroll-saw blade (Illus. 8, top). Bore out the ⅜″-diameter pull-cord hole and rub all the cut

edges down with the graded sandpaper. Aim for a smooth, slightly round-edged finish. Finally, cut the two cam shapes, glue them together, drill out the axle hole, and sand to a good finish.

Making the Side Plates

Look at Illus. 2 again and see how the side plates function not only as supports for the axles and the through-duck pivot but also as coverups for the ends of the pivot and as "waves." Note how, at 6½″ in length and ¼″ in thickness, the plates are paired at each side of the chassis and fitted in the recesses with round-head screws. See, also, how there are two small plates and two large plates.

Trace off a single "large" side profile, pencil-press the traced lines through to the working face of the ¼″-thick plywood, and then use the scroll saw to achieve four identical "large" plates. Strap the four identical plates together with masking tape, establish the position of

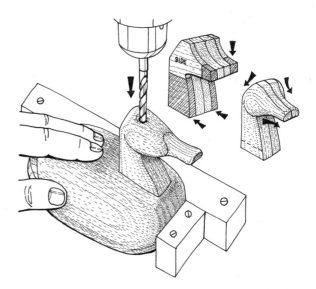

Illus. 7. Top right: Remove the shaded areas of waste with a saw, and then use the knife to whittle and model the head, working with small thumb-paring strokes. Bottom: Secure the duck by pushing it up against a bench stop, and make sure that the drill runs through the duck at right angles to the base line.

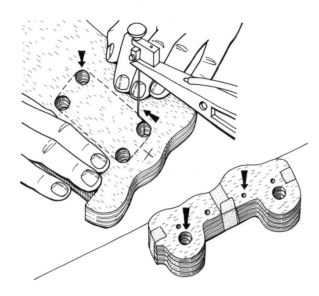

Illus. 8. Top: Drill four ⅜″-diameter holes at the corners of the cam holes, and use one of the holes as an entry point for the scroll-saw blade. Bottom: Make a sandwich of the four side plates, and strap it together with masking tape. Then drill the ½″-diameter axles holes and the ⅛″-diameter screw holes.

the ½″-diameter axle holes and the ⅛″-diameter screw holes, and then bore the holes straight through the four-thickness sandwich (Illus. 8, bottom). When this is done, separate the four plates and reduce two of them down using the "small" waves pattern. Take the two larger plates and bore out the through-duck pivot holes.

Pair the side plates up so that you have a small and large plate at either side of the chassis. Have the smaller plates arranged and set to the outside so that they cover up the through-duck pivot holes.

Turning the Wheels

Study Illus. 2 once more and see how the wheels are turned on the lathe using a four-jaw chuck. Of course, you could do without the chuck and turn the wheels between centers and part off with a saw, but the chuck not only makes the roughing out and parting off that much easier, but it also enables you to turn each wheel with one perfect face.

Check to make sure that the lathe is in good working condition, arrange all your tools so that they are comfortably close at hand, and mount the 10″ length of prepared 3 × 3″-square wood between the chuck and the tailstock center. With the wood well mounted and the tool rest positioned just a fraction below center height, use a round-nosed gouge to swiftly turn the wood down to a 2½″-diameter cylinder. Use the skew chisel to bring the wood to a smooth finish. Take the ruler and dividers and, working from left to right and allowing for, say, 1½″ of waste at the chuck, set the wood out with alternating ½″ and 1″ step-offs. Reckon on making five 1″-thick wheels, with a ½″ of waste between each wheel. This will give you an extra wheel, just in case you make a mistake.

When you have marked out the 2½″-diameter cylinder with all the step-offs that go into making up the design, take the parting tool and sink all the between-wheel waste areas in to a depth of an inch. This should leave you with a ½″-diameter core of waste. Use the point of the skew chisel to face each wheel with a central V-section line and to turn off the sharp edges (Illus. 9, top).

Having achieved what you consider are five nicely matched wheels, move the tailstock well out of the way and reposition the tool rest so that it is over the bed of the lathe and you can work the cylinder end on. With the wood now held in the jaws of the chuck, take the skew chisel and cut back the end-cylinder waste, until you come to the face of the first wheel. When you get down to the working face, bring the wheel to a good smooth finish, tidy up the details, mark the center, and then very carefully part off (Illus. 9, bottom). And so you continue cutting back the core of waste, facing up the wheel, marking the center, parting off, and then moving on to the next wheel, until you have five wheels. Finally, use the drill and the ⅜″-diameter bit to bore out the axle holes.

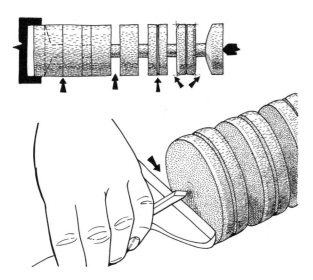

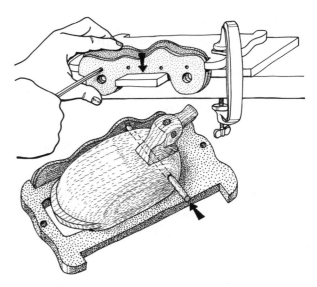

Illus. 9. Top: Mark off the 2½″-diameter cylinder with all the step-offs that go into making up the design. Sink the between-wheel waste, and use the skew chisel to set each wheel "tire" out with a central V-section line. Turn off the sharp edges. Bottom: Clean up the face of the wheel, mark the center-point, and part off.

Illus. 10. Top: Cut a T-shaped jig to support the side plates, secure the base in position on the jig, hold the side plates against the base, and attach with screws. Bottom: Slide the dowel through the duck, place the duck on the base, and run the dowel-ends into the side-plate pivot holes.

Painting and Putting the Piece Together

Having made all the parts that compose the toy—the duck, the chassis base, the side plates, the wheels, the cam, the four washers, and the various dowels—move them to the area set aside for painting and set out all your painting materials. As to colors, it's best to go for a natural clear-varnish finish for the duck and simple bold primary colors for the base and wheels. You might paint the wheels bright red, the chassis base dark blue, the side plates two shades of light blue, and so on. Leave the cam, washers, and axles unpainted, and clean paint away from holes intended for moving parts.

When the paint is completely dry, establish the length of the axles and the position of the cam on the drive axle. Note: Allow ¹⁄₁₆″ extra between the chassis and the wheels for easy movement. Screw one set of side plates into position (Illus. 10, top), and then slide the

dowel through the duck and glue it in place. When the glue is dry, set the dowel-end in the side-plate pivotal hole (Illus. 10, bottom). When this is done, screw the other set of side plates into position so that both ends of the through-duck pivot are held and secured. The duck should now be sitting flat on the base and securely pivoted between the side plates.

Take the drive axle, and slide it through one side-plate hole, through the cam, and on through the other side plate. Make sure that the cam is set centrally within the cam-drive hole, and glue both the wheels and the cam in position on the axle. Finally, fit and attach the other axle and wheels as well as the pull-cord. Now the toy is finished and ready to go.

Hints and Modifications

● When you are in the final stages of working the duck with the rasp, knife, and sandpaper, try to achieve smooth-flowing lines between the neck and body, as if the form had been made from a single block of wood.

- The relationship between the curve of the cam, the size of the chassis hole, and the shape of the duck is critical. If the cam catches and sticks on either the back of the duck or the cam hole, be ready to adjust the shape of the cam and/or the curve of the duck's underside.
- If you like the overall project but want to avoid wood turning, then either use ready-made plastic wheels or adjust the project slightly and make plywood wheels on the scroll saw.

- If, when you come to making the wheels on the lathe, you use the four-jaw chuck, as described, make sure that the wood is perfectly secure before you remove the tailstock.
- You could extend the project by making several ducklings. You could tie or hook them together on the back so that they appear to be swimming in a line behind the mother duck.
- If you don't have a scroll saw, then use a bow saw to cut out the duck and a fretsaw or a coping saw for the plywood.

4

PULL-ALONG PENDULUM HORSES AND FIGURES

A swinging-pendulum toy with horses and figures, painted with traditional fairground imagery

Primary techniques: turning between centers, turning on a screw chuck, split turnings, whittling, and freehand painting

Illus. 1. Project picture.

Characterized by its beautiful turnings—the tapered pillars with their ball finials, the strong-necked part-circle horses' heads, the charming little figures, the powerful half-disc pendulum, and the wheels—this is an amazingly ingenious folk toy.

The toy is a much-loved classic, drawing its inspiration from the whole gamut of turned, carved, and painted wooden-horse toys that were made in the eighteenth and nineteenth centuries in the German districts of Thuringia, Nuremberg, Omerammergau, and Berchtesgaden.

German folk toys of this type are not only known for their imaginative and exciting use of woodworking techniques but also for their economic use of time and materials. The pendulum and the horses' heads can be cut from the same turning, the little arms and legs are made from split turnings, the pillars, wheels, and mushroom-stub axles can be turned all of a piece, and so on.

What toddler wouldn't find pleasure in a toy that can be wheeled, whirled, and wobbled—a toy with little riders who wave their arms and legs in pure delight as they are dragged,

53

swinging and galloping, across the carpeted prairies of the playroom floor. And as for the toymaker, there's pleasure to be taken in the boldness of the designs, the skill-stretching techniques, the directness of the forms, and the look on the child's face when he is handed the completed toy.

Design and Technique Considerations

Study Illus. 2 and 3 and see how the greater part of the toy is made on the lathe. Consider how the wonderfully direct dynamism of the

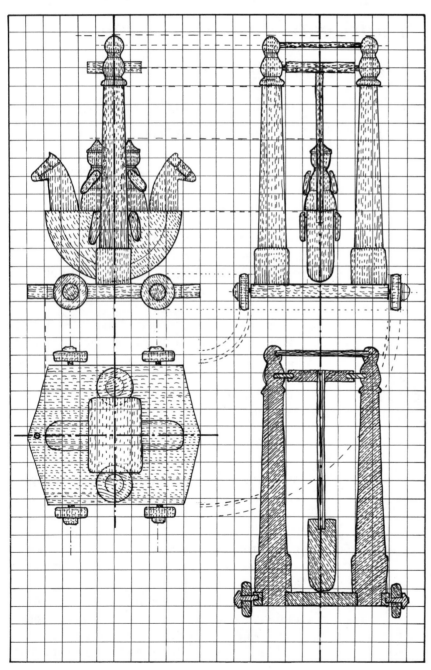

Illus. 2. Working drawings. The scale is one grid square to 1″.

toy hinges on the fact that the pendulum and the horses' heads are turned and cut from the same piece of wood. Of course, you could modify the design and have the toy fretted from flat wood rather than turned, but it would be a pity. In this case, it's best to work within the spirit of the old German toymakers.

Now look at Illus. 5 and 7 and note how the various turnings are designed and worked—the two pillars with their ball-top finials, the disc for the horses and the pendulum, the two figures, the limbs, the four wheels, and the four mushroom-stub axles. Consider the way it is possible to economize on time and mate-

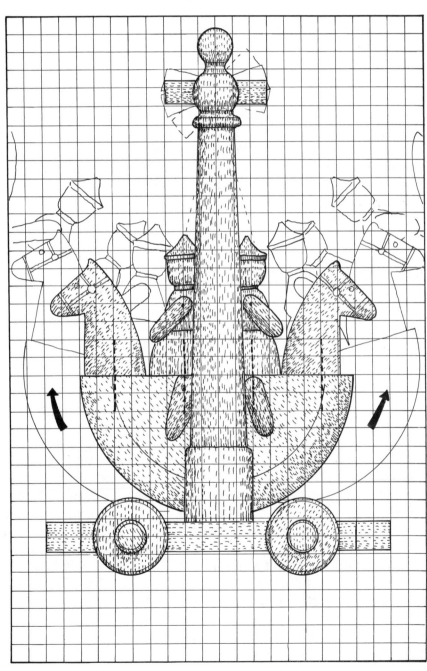

Illus. 3. Working drawing. The scale is two grid squares to 1".

rials by grouping various elements and turning them from the same piece of wood. For example, the two figures can be worked together, the limbs and the axle stubs can be worked from the same turning, the pillars and the wheels could likewise be turned together, and so on. It's best to measure your lathe—the distance between centers and the over-bed swing—and then to plan out your order of work accordingly.

The horses' heads and the little figures do need to be whittled, but the cuts are all swift and uncomplicated. The figures are cut away at the back and the horses' heads from the front.

When you come to choosing your wood, make sure that you select an easy-to-turn wood like beech. Finally, note how the whole project is put together; there are no potentially dangerous nails or screws, just glue and pegs!

Tools and Materials

- A plank of prepared ¾"-thick wood that is 11" long and 8½" wide—for the base (this allows for wastage).
- A 36" length of 2½ × 2½"-square beech—for the two pillars.
- A 12" length of 2 × 2"-square beech—for the two figures.
- A 2"-thick slab of beech at 9 × 9" square—for the pendulum and the horses' heads.
- A 12" length of 2½ × 2½"-square beech—for the wheels and stub axles.
- A length of ¾"-thick beech that is 5" long and 3" wide—for the seesaw bar on top of the pendulum.
- A 12" length of 1 × 1"-square beech—for the limbs.
- A 24" length of ½"-diameter dowel—for the various rods.
- The use of a lathe with a screw chuck.
- The use of a workbench.
- Work-out and tracing paper.
- A pencil and ruler.
- A good selection of wood-turning tools.
- A pair of compasses and callipers.

- A straight saw.
- A hand drill with a selection of bits to fit.
- A pack of graded sandpapers.
- A quantity of PVA glue.
- A selection of broad and fine-point paint brushes.
- Acrylic paints in colors to suit.
- A can of clear high-gloss yacht varnish.
- All the usual workshop items, such as old cloths, off-cuts, bits of dowel, etc.

Setting Out and Making the Base Slab

When you have a good clear understanding of how the turnings need to be worked and precisely how the toy needs to be made and put together, spread your chosen lengths of wood out on the bench and check them over for possible problems. Having made sure that the wood is free from knots, splits, stains, and the like, check each piece for size and generally clear your workshop area.

Take the prepared 11 × 8½" slab of wood—the wood for the base—and mark in the best face and center-lines. Use a pencil, ruler, and square to establish the width, length, and shape of the pointed ends. When this is done, take the straight saw and cut away the small areas of waste at the sides and end-corners. When you have achieved a nice crisp point-ended slab, use the graded sandpapers to rub the wood down to a smooth, slightly round-edged finish.

With the base slab now being 10" long and 8" wide, take a look at Illus. 2 and see how the two pillars are set on the center-line and positioned so that they are 5½" apart between centers. Note, also, how the wheels are set 2½" in from each end of the base. Having clearly established the position of the two pillars and the wheels, mark in the center-point placings of the bottom-of-pillar spigots and the wheel stubs.

When you have double-checked that all is correct, take the hand drill and bore out the spigot and stub-axle holes. It's best if the spigot holes are between ¾ and 1½″ in diameter and the stub-axle holes are ⅜″ in diameter. Make sure that all holes are at right angles to the face of the wood.

Turning the Pillars

Study Illus. 2 and see how the pillars are about 15″ long from the top of the finial ball to the bottom of the through-base spigot, 2″ in diameter at the base, slightly tapered along their length, and set out at the top with a bead and two balls. Note the distance of 12″ from the slab base through to the pendulum-swing center. Draw the pillar profile up to size and take tracings.

Having made sure that the lathe is in good safe working condition, take the 36″ length of 2½ × 2½″-square wood and establish the end-centers by drawing crossed diagonals.

Note: If you have a small lathe, you might need to cut the wood in half and work the two pillars as separate turnings.

Now mount the wood between lathe centers and adjust the tailstock so that the workpiece is secure. If you are working with a dead-center tailstock, ease it back half a turn and oil the spin-hole. Set the tool rest as close as possible to the work and slightly below lathe-center height.

Switch on the power and use a round-nosed gouge to swiftly cut the wood back to a smooth, cylindrical section. Aim for a diameter of about 2¼″. When you have achieved such a section, take the ruler and dividers and carefully set out the various measurements that make up the design. So, from left to right along the wood, step off the measurements for the first pillar: 3″ for end waste, ¾″ for the through-base spigot, 2″ for the pillar base, or bed, 9″ for the long taper, ½″ for the top-of-taper bead, 1½″ for the large ball, and finally 1¼″ for the finial ball (Illus. 4, top). When you have stepped off the first pillar, reverse the measurements and continue marking out the

step-offs for the second pillar in like manner. Note: If you have the two pillars together head to head, you will find it easier to compare and match up the forms.

Having clearly marked in the position of the various step-offs with either the point of the dividers or a pencil, take a thin parting tool and register the depth of the various hollows by sinking pilot cuts. Be careful to sink the cuts either directly on the mark or on the waste side, as the case might be. Work along the wood, setting out all the diameters that make up the design. For example, as the diameter of the spigot needs to match the diameter of the base hole, say, 1″, then the sinking on the turning at that point needs to be cut in so that the remaining bottom-of-sinking diameter is 1″.

Take the tool of your choice—you might use a small round-nosed gouge or a skew chisel—and turn away the waste. The spigot, the pillar base, and the various beads and balls at the top of the pillar are easy enough, but when you come to the 9″-long taper, then you might have problems. Because of its relatively slender length, it might be necessary to steady the work with your fingers, using your thumb only to hold down the tool. It's best to work the top and bottom of the pillar first and then to

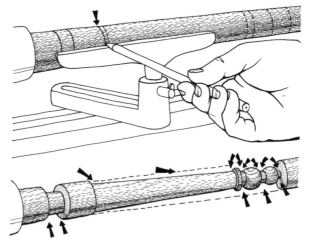

Illus. 4. Top: Stepping off the measurements for the pillar. Bottom: Use a skew chisel to turn off the profile, in the direction of the grain.

turn the taper to fit. Use a skew chisel and work the taper from high to low wood, meaning from the wide base and along through to the slender top (Illus. 4, bottom). Once you have turned both pillars to a nicely matched and sanded finish, part off and remove the wood from the lathe.

Turning the Disc for the Pendulum and the Horses

First take a look at Illus. 5 and then mount your chosen screw chuck on the lathe, making sure that it is secure. Take the 2″-thick, 9 × 9″-square slab of beech, and establish the center point by drawing crossed diagonals. Adjust the compass to a radius of 4″, and set the wood

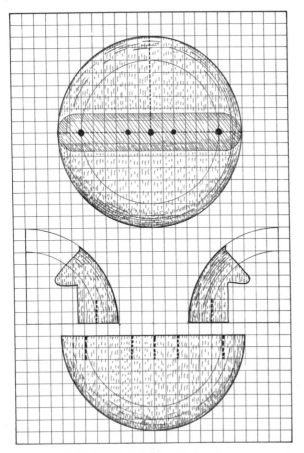

Illus. 5. Working drawings—details for the turned-and-carved horses. Scale: two grid squares to 1″.

out with an 8″-diameter circle. Take the hand drill and the ⅛″-diameter bit, and run a pilot hole through the center of the circle. Use the straight saw to cut away the bulk of the corner waste.

Mount the roughed-out blank on the screw chuck, move the tailstock well out of the way, and bring the tool rest up so that you can approach the wood face on. Switch on the lathe and swiftly turn off the face until it is smooth and slightly rippled. Do one face and then turn the wood over and do the other. Aim to equalize both sides and reduce the overall thickness to about 1½″. When this is done, resituate the tool rest so that you can approach the disc edge on. Being very wary not to dig the tool too deep, carefully turn off the edge of the wood until you have a square-edged disc at about 8¼″ in diameter. When you have achieved such a disc, take the skew chisel and turn off the sharp corners (Illus. 6). Aim for a round-edged disc that is 8″ in diameter.

Move the disc of wood to the bench. Now take another look at Illus. 5 and see how the disc needs to be cut down so as to make a half-disc for the pendulum and two quarter-discs for the horses' heads. First run a straight saw-cut through the center of the disc so as to achieve the two half-circles, and then use a flat surface and a try square to establish the quarters. Use a straight saw to cut the quarters. Making sure that the curve of the horse's mane or neck is nicely aligned with the curve of the disc, trace off the horse's head and pencil-press-transfer the profile through to the quarter-discs. When you are satisfied that all is correct and as described, take the coping saw and cut out the two horse profiles. When you are sawing, be careful in holding and maneuvering the saw so that the blade passes through the wood at right angles to the working face.

Take a knife and whittle away the sides of the horse until the wood angles in from the edge of the curve through to the forehead, nose, and neck. Aim to reduce the wood down to a square-ended–wedge thickness of about a ¼″ (Illus. 6, bottom). Then remove the small V-shaped piece of waste from between the ears.

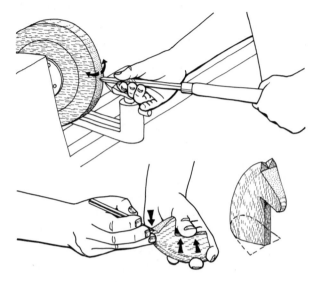

Illus. 6. Top: Take the skew chisel and turn off the sharp corners. Bottom: Whittle away the sides of the horse's neck and nose, and make a V-shaped cut between the ears.

Turning the Figures and Limbs

With a clear understanding of how the figures need to be turned and worked (Illus. 7), take the 12″ length of 2 × 2″-square wood and check it over for possible flaws. If the wood is smooth, of a good color, and free from splits and knots, then you have no problem. Establish the end center-points by drawing crossed diagonals, and then set the ends out with 2″-diameter circles. Draw tangents at the circles' diagonal crossover points, and establish the areas of corner waste by drawing lines from the resultant octagons and along the length of the wood. Use a plane or rasp to clear the bulk of the waste.

Secure the wood between lathe centers, and use the round-nosed gouge to swiftly turn the wood down to a round section. Don't try too hard to achieve a perfect surface; just settle

for a smooth cylinder that is about 2″ in diameter.

Now, allowing for a couple of inches or so at each end for waste, use a pencil, ruler, and dividers to set off the various lengths that make up the little figures (Illus. 7, left). So,

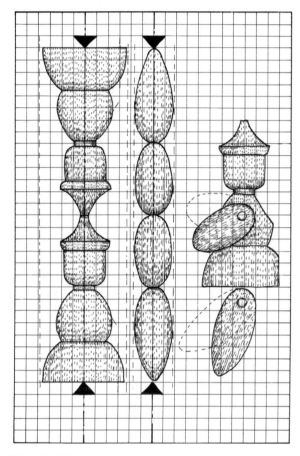

Illus. 7. Working drawings—details for the turned-and-carved figures. Scale: four grid squares to 1″.

from left to right, have ⅞″ for the dress, 1⅛″ for the chest, ⅛″ for the neck, ¾″ for the head, and ¾″ for the hat. Having stepped off the measurements for one figure, reverse and repeat the step-offs for the second figure. Note: Turning the figures head to head makes for easier comparisons when you come to matching up shapes and profiles.

Check to make sure that all the step-offs are correct, and then take a slender parting tool and sink all the pilot cuts that go into making up the design. For example, the step-off point that marks the position of the waist needs to be sunk to a depth of about ½" so as to leave you with a waist diameter of slightly over an inch. And the step-off that marks the position of the neck needs to be sunk to a depth of nearly ¾" to leave you with a neck diameter of ½". However, if you are using a thick parting tool and if the step-off indicates a tight V-cut valley, like with the waist, then don't sink the pilot cut quite so deep.

When you have marked and cut all the hollows that make up the design, take the skew chisel and carefully turn off all the waste. Don't be in too much of a hurry to cut down to the envisaged form; it's much better to take it little by little, gradually easing out the waste. As you are turning, always angle the tool so as to cut with the grain, that is, from peaks to hollows, or from high wood down to low wood. When you have turned off the two figures, run through a final skim with the chisel to bring the wood to a crisp smooth finish and then part off and remove the wood from the lathe.

Look at Illus. 7 and see how the backs are

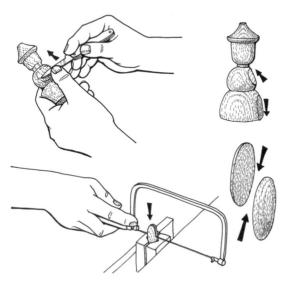

Illus. 8. Top: Hold the figure securely in one hand, and use carefully controlled knife strokes to remove the waste. Bottom: Secure the turnings in the vise, and use the coping saw to achieve the small "split" limbs.

cut away. Work on one piece at a time. Holding the figure in one hand so that the head end is farthest away, use a sharp knife to slice away the curve of wood from the waist to the neck (Illus. 8, top). Now turn the figure over so that the head is facing you, and remove the wood at the back of the skirt with a couple of carefully controlled cuts.

Note: Should the knife slip, you run the risk of cutting away the back of the head and the brim of the hat, so be careful!

The limbs are pretty straightforward; all you do is inspect and prepare the wood, as already described, and then turn the limbs between centers. Of course, the turnings are small and rather delicate, so you do have to work with care, but, other than that, the profiles are swift and easy to turn. When you have turned off the four shapes, split them down their length with the coping saw so that you have four arms and four legs (Illus. 8, bottom).

Turning the Wheels and Mushroom-Stub Axles

Look back at Illus. 2 and note that, in addition to the pillars and the figures, the wheels and the stub axles are also turned.

The wheels are best turned between centers, in much the same way as you turned the figures. Prepare and mount the wood, as with the figures, and swiftly clear away the waste; then step off the wheel thicknesses along the cylinder. The shaping is easy enough; you start by sinking a pilot cut between each wheel and then you round off the shoulders and part off. However, the wheels are open to all manner of interpretation. You might have big chunky wheels, or almost-round balls, or wheels that appear to have tires, and so on. Then again, you could modify the project slightly by buying a set of four plastic wheels. It needs some consideration.

The mushroom-stub axles are only a problem in that they are small. Mount the prepared wood between centers as already described, step off the various measurements that make up the design, sink the various pilot cuts, and then turn off the waste. Bear in mind that the stubs do need to be a precise length and width. For instance, the stubs need to pass through the wheels for a loose easy fit, and yet at the same time they must be a tight friction-fit in the holes that are drilled in the edges of the base. The easiest option is to go for base holes at ⅜″ in diameter, stubs at ⅜″ in diameter, and the wheel holes drilled out to ½″. As for shape and uniformity, the best procedure is to turn off at least six turnings and then to choose the four that are best matched.

Putting the Piece Together

You should now have the base all cut and drilled, the two pillars, the four wheels, the four stub axles, the two figures, the four arms, the four legs, the half-disc pendulum, a length of wood for the seesaw pivot at the top of the pendulum, and various lengths and sizes of dowel. Take a pencil and label all the pieces.

Start by taking the half-disc, the horses' heads, and the figures, and marking in all the attachment holes. In the sawn face, or edge, of the half-disc, sink a ½″-diameter hole at dead center for the pendulum shaft and ⅛″-diameter peg-attachment holes for each of the horses and figures. Each horse and figure requires a corresponding ⅛″-diameter peg attachment hole in its base. Reckon on having all peg holes about an inch deep. The easiest procedure is to first secure the pendulum in the vise, drill the various holes (Illus. 9, left), put little pegs in the drill holes, and finally drill the horses and figures to fit the pendulum-peg positions.

Dry-fit the figures and horses to the pendulum (Illus. 9, right); then fit the main pendulum shaft. Now drill and peg the arms on the figures, and the legs on the pendulum, so that they are a swinging fit. Have the pegs a loose fit through the figure and pendulum

holes, and a tight fit through the limbs (Illus. 10, top left).

The two units at the top of the pillars are a little more tricky. With the two pillars in place on the base, drill, peg, and fit the seesaw plank so that it is pivoted between the pillar finials (Illus 10, bottom). Note that you will have to remove and replace the pillar. Aim for an easy swing fit. When this is done, drill out the plank at face-center and fit the pendulum shaft. If all is well, the pendulum, complete with horses and figures, should swing in a smooth arc and just clear the base. When you are pleased with the fit, remove the pillars from the base, drill the top-inside finial balls, and fit and attach the linking dowel. The dowel has two functions: It holds the top of the pillars a set distance apart, and it stops the pendulum-seesaw plank from swinging right over and out of control.

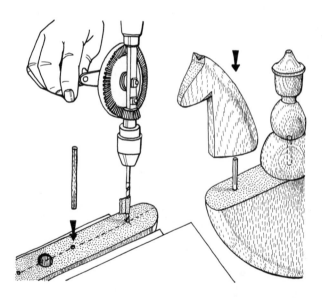

Illus. 9. Left: Put the pendulum in the vise and drill out the various peg holes. Right: Drill holes in the base of the horses and figures; then have a dry-run fitting.

Finally, once you have brought all the elements together in a good dry fit, knock them apart and clear your work area in readiness for painting.

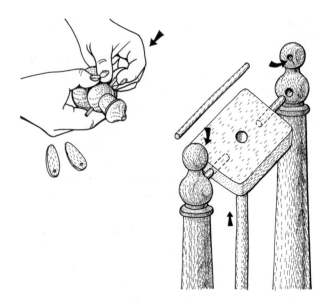

of the base color, with a light sanding after the first coat.

When your base, or ground, colors are dry, then comes the exciting part of painting all the patterns, motifs, and details that go into making up the design. Use a fine-point brush to highlight the features on the figures and horses, the barley-twist pattern up the pillars, and the pattern on the wheels. Spend time getting it just right. The good thing is that if you do make a mistake, all you do is wipe it away before it dries, redo the ground color, and start over again. When all of the paint is dry, lay on a couple of coats of varnish.

Finally, fit, glue, and peg the toy together, and then knot and attach the pull-rope, and the toy is finished.

Illus. 10. Top left: Make sure that the pegs are a loose fit through the figure and a tight fit through the limbs. Bottom: Drill and fit the seesaw plank and the pendulum, and then fit the linking dowel at the top of the pillars.

Painting and Finishing

When you are basically pleased with the way all the parts fit together, wipe them over with a damp cloth to remove all the dust and then set out your brushes and paints and generally prepare your work area for painting. Work out an arrangement—a rack or line—for supporting the pieces while the paint is drying. Bear in mind that if by mistake you paint close-fitting areas that are best left unpainted, you will have to rub back to the wood.

Take a look at the project picture (Illus. 1) and the painting grid (Illus. 11). We have chosen to use bright bold colors: green for the base, red for the figures and the wheels, and so on. Decide on the colors you want to use and on how many items are going to be painted the same color, and then plan the working order accordingly. Bearing in mind that acrylics dry almost as fast as you put them on, try to give all units two well-brushed coats

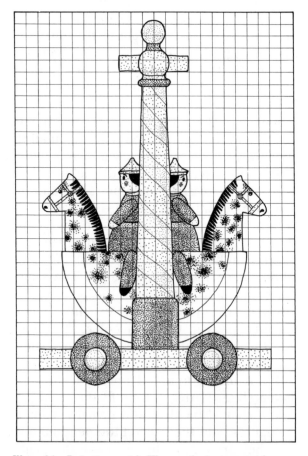

Illus. 11. Painting grid. The scale is two grid squares to 1″.

62

Hints and Modifications

- Although we suggest turning the pillars, the wheels, and the mushroom-stub axles from different lengths of wood, there's no reason why you couldn't modify the project and turn several items all of a piece. Certainly, this way of working can be wasteful in that you have to turn off more wood, but, then again, you don't have so much end-center waste nor do you have to spend so much time setting up the lathe.

- If you want to go for more complex forms, you could hollow-turn the faces of the disc and have, say, a series of beads and hollows running up the pillars.

- When you are choosing your wood, it's best to select an easy-to-turn, smooth-grained wood like beech, cherry, or sycamore; I prefer beech.

- Always protect your work from bruising by muffling the jaws of the vise with soft wood or felt.

- We have chosen to use wooden pins for the primary attachments because they are relatively safe and child-proof. Don't use nails. If you do decide to use screws rather than wooden pins, make sure that they are made of brass.

- When gluing a dowel or peg into a hole, make two small grooves along the dowel to provide a space, or "key," for a more secure attachment.

- Bearing in mind that this is a toy for a toddler, it's most important for all the materials to be safe and nontoxic. The paint needs to be acrylic, the wood must be splinter-resistant, and, as much as possible, all sharp edges and corners should be rubbed down and slightly rounded.

5
A SIT-ON, PULL-ALONG HORSE

A knight's horse with wheels, big enough for a toddler

Primary techniques: built-up, fretted, shaped, and painted with knight's charger imagery

When I was a kid in the '50s, I used to dream about knights in armor, sword fights, and riding about on a fierce charger. One of my favorite games was to hang a sack full of grass cuttings over the fence and sit astride the bulging bag as if it were a horse. It didn't do the fence much good and I wasn't very popular with the neighbors, but, despite all that, it was really good fun. Using pieces of old rope for stirrups and reins, I would happily gallop through a fantasy world peopled with all manner of Errol Flynn– and Tony Curtis–inspired black-and-white knights.

I reckon that this pull-along push-along, sit-on toy horse beats my stuffed sack any day. And with its smooth, arched, polished-wood saddle, brightly painted flanks, stirrup brackets, rope tail, and painted armor, it is bound to be a hit with most tube-watching toddlers today.

If you like building larger projects and painting, and if you know of a toddler who has a yen for horses, then this project could well be a winner.

Design and Technique Considerations

Take a look at the working drawings (Illus. 2) and the diagrammatic cutting grid (Illus. 3), and see how, at a grid scale of one square to

Illus. 1. Project picture.

1", the horse is about 19" high from the ground line to the top of the head, 20" long from nose to tail, and 16" wide across the span of the wheels. See how the body of the horse is built bridgelike, with the arched end-boards supporting the saddle seat and with the laminated head being mortised through the seat and screwed to the front board. Consider how the use of best-quality, 1"-thick multicore plywood lessens the need for complex joinery and internal support struts. Note the fretted double-thickness head, the strong and yet light-weight base board, and the various pull/push hand slots and rope holes.

All in all, this toy is fancy enough to keep most children happy, while at the same time the techniques are such that it can easily be built, even by beginners.

Tools and Materials

- A sheet of best-quality, 1″-thick, birch-faced multicore plywood at about 36 × 36″—this allows for waste.
- Eight 12″ lengths of prepared white pine that is ½″ thick and about 2″ wide—for the flank boards, four at either side of the horse.
- A 12′ length of 1 × 1″-square wood—for the various internal attachment battens, the stirrup bar, and the axle blocks.
- A length of straight-grained, knot-free pine that is 12″ long, 8″ wide, and 3″ thick—for the saddle seat.
- A 4′ length of soft-cotton–covered rope—for the reins.
- A 12″ length of ¾″-thick rope— for the tail.
- A quantity of brass screws that are ¾″, 1½″, and 2″ long, some with countersunk and others with round heads—for the various attachments.
- Four 4″-diameter, heavy-duty, solid-face plastic wheels with rubber tires—to fit ⅜″-diameter axles.
- Two 16″ lengths of ⅜″-diameter mild steel rods, with end clips, brass washers, and chrome or plastic dome caps to fit (at the end of each axle, there are a couple of brass washers, the wheel, a patent star-ring clip, and a chrome or plastic dome).
- Several large sheets of tracing and work-out paper.
- A pencil, compass, and ruler.
- The use of a large bench with a vise.
- A coping saw.
- A scroll saw—we use a Hegner.

- A flat straight saw.
- A set of C-clamps.
- A hand drill with bits at 1″, ¾″, ½″, ⅜″, and ¼″ diameter.
- A hand plane.
- A mallet and a 2″-wide mortise chisel.
- An open-toothed, Surform type of rasp.
- A quantity of white PVA wood glue.
- Two large brass screw-eyes—for the reins.
- A selection of acrylic paints in colors to suit.
- A can of clear yacht varnish.
- All the usual workshop items, such as brushes, sandpaper, screwdrivers, old cloths, and brush cleaners.

Setting Out the Wood and Cutting the Profiles

Sit down with your pencil, ruler, and work-out paper, and draw the design up to full size. When you have studied Illus. 2 and 3 and decided how you want your horse to be—perhaps you want it larger, made out of different materials, or whatever—set out all your materials and check them over to make sure that everything is correct. Is the timber free from splits, warps, and knots? Do the wheels fit the axles? Are your chosen screws long enough? All these points need to be considered at the start of the project. Now, having spent time making sure that the measurements are correct, draw in the center-line and check for symmetry. It's most important that the base and the end-boards be set square and symmetrical. Double-check with your drawings and layouts to make sure that the design, as you have drawn it, is going to work out.

When you are sure that everything is correct, trace off the design and pencil-press-transfer the traced lines through to the working face of the 1″-thick plywood. Use a compass, ruler, and square to adjust and finalize the shape of the curves and the position of the various slots, holes, and cutouts. When you are drawing in the profiles, pay particular attention to the top curves of the two end-boards and the inner curves of the base board

(Illus. 4, top). Having established the designs and shapes with crisp clear clean-cut lines, set to work with the scroll and the straight flat saw, cutting out the forms and profiles. Use the straight saw for the long straight sides and the scroll saw for curves and profiles. Make sure that the under-jaw head slots are a square-edged tight fit over the 1″-ply thickness of the front board. When you have made the five plywood cutouts—the two horses' heads, the two end-boards, and the base board—glue and clamp the two heads together to make a single 2″ thickness (Illus. 4, bottom).

When the glue is dry, take the plane, rasp, and graded sandpapers, and work all the sawn plywood edges so that they are appropriately

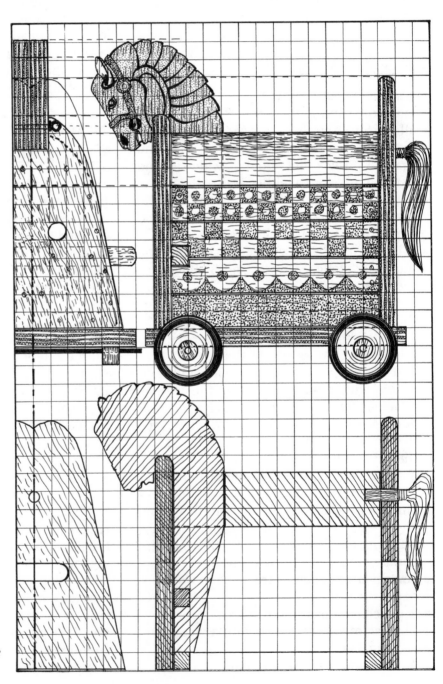

Illus. 2. Working drawings. The scale is one grid square to 1″.

square or rounded. For example, the bottom edges of the end-boards need to be crisply square-cut, whereas all the inside and outside edges of the base board need to be slightly rounded. And the outer edges of the end-boards need to be fully rounded (Illus. 5, top left and center), but the laminated horse's head needs to be square-cut where it hooks

over the top of the end-board and is screwed flush to the inside face of the end-board (Illus. 5, top right). You will have to square off and trim the top-edge curve of the front board to fit the head and neck.

Once you have worked all the plywood cutouts to a good finish, take another refresher look at the working drawings (Illus. 2) so that

Illus. 3. Diagrammatic cutting grid. The scale is one grid square to 1".

67

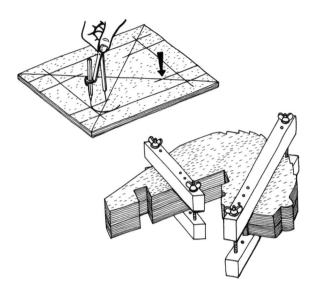

Illus. 4. Top: Use a compass, ruler, and try square to mark out the straight lines and curves that go into making up the base board. Bottom: Glue and clamp the two horses' head profiles together to make a single 2″ thickness.

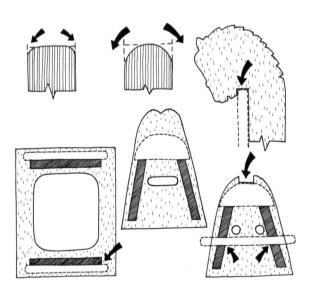

Illus. 5. Top left and center: The inside and outside edges of the base board and the top edges of the end-board need to be slightly rounded. Top right: Leave the plywood square-edged where it hooks over and meets the front end-board. Bottom, left to right: The shaded areas show the position of the 1″-wide attachment battens, the base, and the back and front ends.

you are clear as to how the boards relate to one to another, and then draw in the position of the various 1″-wide attachment battens on the base and the inside edges of the end-boards. Leave a gap for the stirrup bar, and set the battens from ⅜ to 1″ in from the edge of the end-board (Illus. 5, bottom).

Making the Saddle Block

Take the 12″-long, 3″-thick, 8″-wide block of straight-grained pine, and check it over to make sure that it is free from splits and loose dead knots. Having made sure that the ends are square-cut, locate the position of the end center-points by drawing crossed diagonals, decide which of the two 12 × 8″ faces of the block is to be "top," and then run a center-line end to end along the wood. Use the tracings to pencil-press-transfer to the 3 × 8″ ends of the wood the arched-bridge shape that makes up the design of the saddle. Shade in the areas that need to be wasted (Illus. 6, bottom left).

Secure the block of wood in the jaws of the vise, and use the plane to cut away the two top corners and sides of waste. Run the plane along the wood—first along one top edge and then along the other—all the while aiming for the beautiful, full, smooth, symmetrical curve that makes up the saddle (Illus. 6, right). When you have cut the curve, take the graded sandpapers and rub the face of the wood down to a silky smooth-to-the-touch finish. It's important for the saddle to be free from splinters and jags (Illus. 7, top left).

Using the end center-lines as reference, reestablish the top-of-the-curve center-line and then use the pencil, ruler, and square to mark in, on the front-top end of the block, the position of the 3″-long, 2″-wide horse's neck mortise slot. Using the center-line as a guide, run the lines that mark out the width of the slot 3″ along the top of the curved saddle and down the full depth of the front end. Make sure that the two lines are 2″ apart, parallel to each

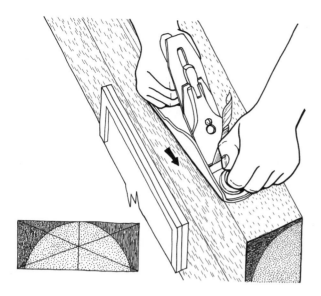

Illus. 6. Bottom left: Draw crossed diagonals to locate the position of the center-line, and then trace off the arched-bridge shape. Shade in the areas to be wasted. Right: Secure the wood in the vise and use the plane to remove the waste. Hold the plane at a slight angle to the cut and push away from the main body. Work from the top of the arch down to the side.

other, and square with the base of the block. When this is done, set the wood end up in the vise (Illus. 7, bottom left) and use the straight flat saw, the coping saw, and the chisel to clear away the waste. If you work a little to the waste side of the drawn line and then skim back slightly with the flat face of the chisel (Illus. 7, right), you will be sure, when you come to fitting the head, of a good push-fit of the neck in the slot.

Putting Together the End-Boards, Saddle, and Axle Blocks

First look back at Illus. 2 and see how the front and back boards are set on the base so that they are about a ½" in from the end-edge and about 1" in from the side edge. When this is done, take the 1 × 1"-square battens, screw them in place on the base, and then screw the end-boards to the battens. It's best to drill

pilot holes through the first thickness—the plywood and/or the battens, as the case might be—and to use countersunk screws on the inside and round-head screws on the outside. When you have mounted the two end-boards on the base, set the saddle-seat block in position between the two boards, support it with battens and clamps (Illus. 8, top left), check for fit, draw in a few guidelines, and then attach with screws. Run the 2"- to 2½"-long screws in from the outside, through the end-boards, and straight on into the body of the saddle block. If all is well, the curve of the saddle should be set back about 1" from the top curved edge of the front board and about ¼" from the side edges. When you are happy with the stability and fit, take the 1 × 1"-square section of wood and, following the pencil-drawn guidelines, screw in the lengths from the base to the saddle along the inside edges

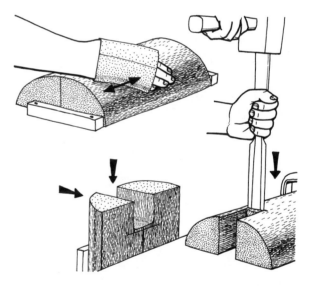

Illus. 7. Top left: The saddle should be smooth and free from splinters. Sand in the direction of the grain, working through the graded sandpapers. It's advisable to use a wrap-around sanding "glove" made from sandpaper and masking tape. Bottom left: Set the wood end up in the vise and use the straight flat saw and the coping saw to clear away the bulk of the waste. Right: Use the 2" chisel to clear the remaining waste. Aim for a tight push-fit.

of the ends. Don't forget to leave a gap for the stirrup bar.

When you are ready to fit the axle blocks, turn back to Illus. 2 and see how they are worked from 3″ lengths of 1 × 1″-square wood. Note how the 3″-long blocks are trenched halfway along their length and screwed to the underside of the base so that they bridge and hold the ⅜″-diameter steel-rod axles in place. The axle blocks don't need to be extra strong, since the weight of the horse bears straight down on the axles; but rather, the function of the blocks is to hold the axles in parallel alignment to each other and to the base board.

Take a 12″ length of 1 × 1″ wood, and use a pencil, ruler, and square to set it out along its length into four 3″ step-offs. Establish the halfway point of each step-off—1½″ along from the end—and then use the coping saw to cut the little ½″-deep, ½″-wide trench that bridges the axle rod. Make sure that all the trenches

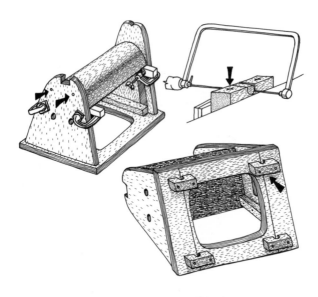

Illus. 8. Top left: Use battens or blocks to support the saddle while it is being attached. Run the screws into the body of the saddle block at the top from the outside of the end-boards. Top right: Hold the axle block in the vise and use the coping saw to remove the ½″-deep trench that bridges the axle rod. Bottom: Screw the axle blocks over the axle center-lines and an inch in from the side edges of the base.

are clean-cut and the same size (Illus. 8, top right). Run screw holes through the blocks—one on each side of the bridge. Now turn the horse frame on its side and mark out the axle center-lines that run across the underside of the base at a point 2½″ in from each end. Bridge the blocks over the line, set them 1″ in from the side edges of the base, and screw them in position (Illus. 8, bottom). Check the blocks for a good smooth axle-fit.

Fitting the Head and the Flank Boards

With the axle blocks screwed into position, turn the horse right-side up and make sure that the neck-mortise hole is free from debris. Have a trial fitting of the head. If all is well, the long neck should slide down through the saddle mortise, to be a close push-fit into the notched top of the end-board. You might need to adjust the joint, until the fit between the underside of the jaw and the end-board is flush and close. When you are pleased with the fit of the head to the body, drill pilot holes in through the front of the end-board and fasten with round-head screws.

Cut the 1 × 1″-square stirrup bar to length—it needs to be slightly shorter than 12″—and round over the ends with the rasp and sandpaper. Slide the bar in from the side of the horse, through the neck hole, and out through the other side of the horse (Illus. 9, top). Make sure that the bar is centered and set parallel to the base board; then fasten it with screws. Run the screws through the end-board and into the bar.

Look once more at Illus. 2 and note how the flanks of the horse are made up of 12″-long, 2″-wide boards—four on each side of the horse. See, also, how the two bottom boards are notched so that they fit over the stirrup bar. Having used the straight saw to cut the boards to size and to work the notches, drill pilot holes at the ends of the boards and screw them to the battens. Make sure that the boards

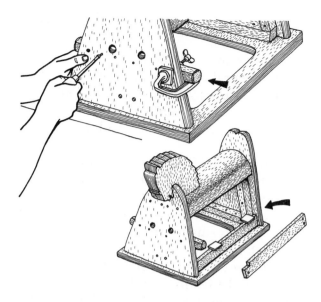

Illus. 9. Top: Slide the stirrup bar in from the side of the horse, through the neck hole, and out of the other side. Make sure that it is centered and parallel to the base board, hold it in place with a clamp, and fasten with screws. Bottom: Use a small piece of scrap wood to space the boards, while screwing them to the battens.

are parallel to the top, to each other, and to the base board, and be sure that there is a small space between each board. Use a small scrap of wood for a spacer, attach the bottom board first, and then repeat the procedure for the other boards (Illus. 9, bottom).

Finishing and Painting

Now turn back to the project picture (Illus. 1) and the working drawings (Illus. 2), and see how the flank boards and the head are painted, while the base, end-boards, and saddle are clear-varnished. When you have studied the details that make up the painted design, trace off the head imagery and press-transfer the traced lines through to the wood. It's best to cut the tracings to fit and to hold them in place with masking tape. Use a ruler and compass to draw in the squares, circles, and scallops that decorate the flank boards (Illus. 10, top left). Make sure that the trans-

ferred lines are clear. When this is done, wipe off all the dust and move the workpiece to the area set aside for painting.

It's best to start with the large areas of color and then to work down to the smaller and still smaller details. So, for example, you might paint the bulk of the head-neck armor a blue-grey, the bottom-flank board (the area underneath the scalloped drape) and alternate squares on the two top-flank boards bright red, and so on (Illus. 10, top right). The joy of using acrylics is that they dry so quickly that colors can easily be layered one on top of another without worrying about the paints running into each other. And so you continue, retracing the details on the head and then painting the eyes, nose, and fine-line details black, the outer eyes and teeth white, and the harness red (Illus. 10, bottom left). When the

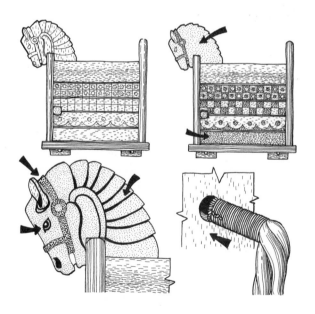

Illus. 10. Top left: Use tracing paper to transfer the horse's head design, and a ruler and compass to draw out the side-panel design. Top right: Paint the horses's head and neck a blue-grey and the side-panel patterns red. Bottom left: Retrace the head design. Paint the details black and use white for the eyes and teeth. Leave the ears natural. Bottom right: Bind and glue the rope tail in the tail hole; then unravel the rope to achieve the full tail.

paint is completely dry, give the whole horse three or four coats of varnish, rubbing down between each coat.

When the varnish is dry, use the ¾″ bit to run the tail hole into the body of the saddle seat and then bind and glue the 12″ length of fat rope in the tail hole. Unravel the rope and tease it out so as to make a beautiful full tail (Illus. 10, bottom right).

Finally, screw the two screw-eyes in place—one at either side of the head—tie on the length of rope to make the reins, or pull-cord, fit the axles, washers, wheels, and patent axles, or wheel attachments, and the horse is ready for its first gallop into battle.

Hints and Modifications

- If you want to create a more naturalistic horse, one with, say, a carved head and a more shapely saddle, use an easy-to-carve wood like lime.
- If you are worried about the horse denting furniture or if you think that the sharp edges of the base may be dangerous, you could attach fenders or bumpers around the edge of the base board—take a look at the next project.
- If you want to build a much larger horse for an older child and decide to double the scale so that the horse is about 24″ wide and 32″ long, there's no problem, as long as you use ½″-diameter axles and, say, 6″-diameter wheels.
- If you want to create a more realistic image, you could use discarded, found, or shop-bought items, such as leather for the reins and stirrups, and leather and felt for a padded saddle.
- If you don't have a scroll saw, you could use either a large coping saw or a bow saw.

6

A SIT-ON, PULL-ALONG WILLY-THE-WHALE TUGBOAT

A skateboard type of boat with caster wheels, rubber fenders, stainless-steel attachments, and a pull-cord

Primary techniques: shaping, dowel-jointing, assembling, and painting

We've all enjoyed water play: making soap bubbles in the kitchen sink, splishing and splashing about in the bath, and later on as we got older, messing about on lakes and rivers. Canoes, rowboats, rafts, ships, yachts, and tugboats—what fun! Most of us have, at some time or other, fantasized about sailing off into the great unknown. As a child, I loved the notion of being cast adrift, of sailing away and finding a desert island, and of chugging along unchartered Amazonian rivers. Water and boats are the stuff of dreams. But, of course, long before many children get to see large bodies of water, they are quite happy to play out their boating fantasies on the safe and untroubled waters of the bedroom carpet. In such play, chairs become boats, beds become tropical islands, and bed covers become billowing waves.

Our Willy-the-Whale tugboat is a great toddler toy. Little ones can sit astride the wheeled boat and trundle it around the playroom or be pulled up and down the garden path—what excitement! Who needs water!

From a woodworker's or toymaker's viewpoint, this toy is special in that, although it can be put together using mostly easy-to-find materials, a few of the materials can only be found at boating chandlers, which makes the design all the more credible.

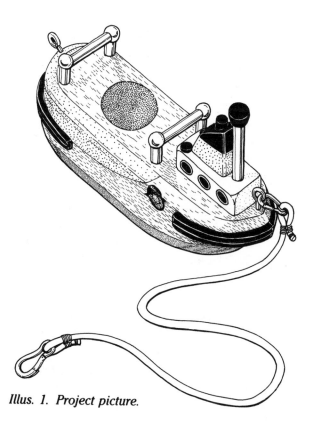

Illus. 1. Project picture.

73

Design and Technique Considerations

Take a good look at Illus. 1 and 2 and see how the tugboat is a pull-along toy in the classic sit-on-and-trundle, go-cart tradition. That is to say, there are a solid base on which to sit or perch and a number of wheels or casters that go in any direction. The toy is designed to be pulled, pushed, trundled, paddled, and scooted, depending upon the age, skill, and inclination of the child. Note how, at a scale of one grid square to 1″, the boat is about 12″ high from the base to the top of the mast, 7″ wide, and 22″ long. Also, note how the shape of the portholes gives the tug its whalelike image.

Now take a look at Illus. 3 and consider the way the toy is put together with glue, stainless-steel tube, and dowels. The project has been designed so that the dowels and tubes are both structural and visual; meaning that not only are the dowels and tubes used to hold the various pieces together, but they are also arranged in such a way that they are seen to be part of the tugboat's superstructure—the mast, the funnel, and the bar stanchions. The base has been set out so that there is a sinking, or bore, hole for each of the four casters. The idea of the strip fender at the stem and stern is so that the lucky child might happily bounce from your Chippendale side table to your Hepplewhite bureau without doing any real damage to his or her person, your collectibles, or, most important of all, the tugboat!

If you like the overall idea of this project but would rather make a speedboat, a barge, or a fishing boat instead, it's easy enough to modify the details accordingly.

Tools and Materials

- A 48″ length of best-quality, prepared, straight-grained, knot-free white pine that is 7″ wide and 3″ thick—for the hull.
- A 12″ length of white pine that is 3″ wide and 1½″ thick—for the cabin and funnel.
- A 24″ length of ¾″-diameter broomstick dowel.
- A 24″ length of ¾″-diameter stainless-steel, chrome, or brass tube—for the deck rails (this allows for a small amount of waste).
- Four stanchions, brackets, posts, or right-angle joints—to fit the tube rails.
- Four small furniture casters or wheels (it's best to use the enclosed-ball type), the smaller the better, with screws to fit.
- A rubber or plastic stop—to fit your tube mast.
- Two large stainless-steel, chrome, or brass screw-eyes.
- A 20″ length of black rubber or plastic fender strip (it's best if the screws are concealed by a colored slide-in strip).
- A 36″ length of rope covered with thick soft cotton, as used on yachts.
- A small amount of strong fine twine—for binding the rope.
- A couple of large boating snap hooks—to fit the screw-eyes and the rope.
- A quantity of white PVA wood adhesive.
- A small quantity of two-tube resin glue.
- A selection of acrylic paints in colors to suit.
- The use of a workbench.
- A straight saw.
- A large, open-toothed, Surform type of wood rasp.
- A couple of large C-clamps.
- The use of a drill press with a long, shanked ¾″-diameter bit and a 2½″-diameter Forstner bit to fit.
- A large pack of graded sandpapers.
- All the usual workshop materials, such as paper, tracing paper, brushes, screwdrivers, masking tape, double-sided transparent tape, paint cans, and old cloths.

Setting Out and Making the Hull

When you have studied the working drawings (Illus. 2 and 3), purchased your prepared wood, and selected all the attachments, set the 48″ length of wood out on the bench and check it over to make sure that it's free from warps, splits, and knots. If the wood contains a loose dead knot or a split that runs into the end grain, then look for another piece. Note: By prepared wood, we mean wood that has either been planed on all faces or at least planed on the broad face.

Use a pencil and square to divide the wood into two 24″ lengths and then use the saw to cut it in half. Take the two halves, hold them up face to face to the light, and see if the mating surfaces are true and square. If all is well, you shouldn't be able to see light shining between the mating surfaces. If, on the other hand, you can see light, then rub one or both of the faces down to remove the high spots.

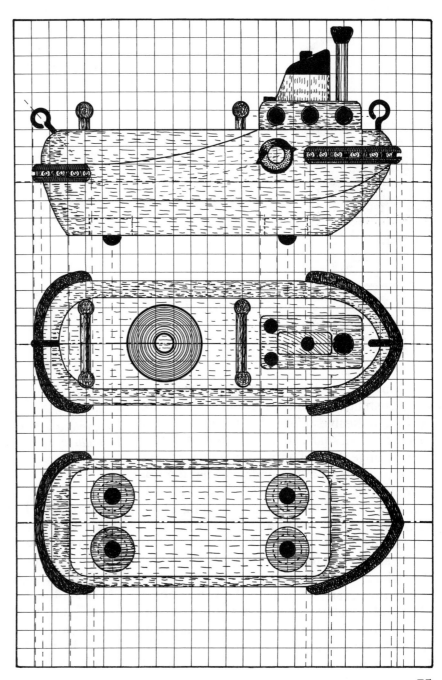

Illus. 2. Working drawings. The scale is one grid square to 1″.

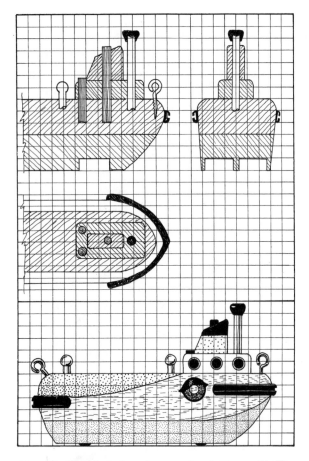

Illus. 3. Working drawings and painting grid. The scale is one grid square to 1".

as to what needs to be cut away. If all is correct and as described, the main prow line should run along the length of the wood at a point about 2" down from the top face. Working on the waste side of the profile lines, take a pencil and ruler and establish straight lines of cut (Illus. 4, top left).

Secure the wood with the "side" face uppermost in the vise, and use the straight saw to cut away the bulk of the waste (Illus. 4, top right and bottom). Don't try to follow the curved profile; just settle for running the saw straight through the wood at right angles to

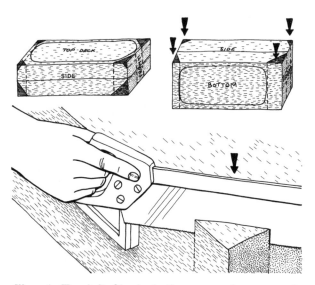

Illus. 4. Top left: Shade in the areas of waste and establish the cutting lines. Top right: Secure the workpiece with the "side" face uppermost, and use the flat straight saw to cut away the bulk of the waste.

Having rubbed the mating faces down to a good flush fit, give both faces a liberal coating of PVA adhesive. Slide the glued surfaces together until movement becomes difficult; then arrange the C-clamps so that they are set about 6" along from the ends and tighten up.

When the glue is set, remove the clamps. You should now have a single 24"-long block of wood that is 7" wide and 6" thick. Take a pencil and label the best 7"-wide face "top deck" and then label all the other faces to fit—the "side," "front," "end," and so on. When this is done, take tracings of the various profiles and carefully pencil-press-transfer the traced lines through to the wood. When you have clearly set out the various views, shade in the areas of waste so that there's no doubt

the working face and for removing the four main corners of waste. When this is done, set strips of double-sided transparent tape on the sawn faces and refit the corners of waste so as to make up the original 24 × 7 × 6" block. Now set the wood in the vise so that the "top deck" face is uppermost, and again cut away all the waste, as can be seen from the top view. Bear in mind that the "top" waste doesn't mark out the shape of the top deck but rather the shape of the tugboat profile at the 2"-from-the-top prow line (Illus. 5, top left). And so you continue, carefully working around the block with the straight saw, removing the four main corners of waste from each face.

Having achieved the basic flat-faced form, clear your work surface of debris and take the rasp and start to work the hull to a smoothly curved finish. Working with and across the grain and starting with the "top deck" profile, run the rasp from the deck profile over and down towards the prow line (Illus. 5, top right and bottom). Don't be in too much of a hurry to finish; it's much better to slowly and carefully achieve a curve here and another curve there, intermittently stopping and comparing the workpiece with the working drawings, until gradually you see the hull taking shape.

When you have what you consider is a good strong hull shape, start to remove the rasp texture with the graded sandpapers. Work from coarse through fine, until the surface becomes smooth and the grain begins to shine (Illus. 6, top left). Now turn the hull over so that the underside is uppermost, establish the position of the four casters or wheels, and then use the drill press and the 2½"-diameter Forstner bit to bore out four flat-bottomed 1"-deep holes (Illus. 6, top right).

Note: You might need to bore out holes of a smaller or larger diameter, depending upon the design and size of your casters or wheels.

Building the Superstructure

When you have finished the hull, put it to one side and take a fresh look at Illus. 3. Note how the cabin and the funnel are made from two blocks of wood, with the funnel mounted on the cabin and the cabin mounted on the deck. See, also, how the two blocks are secured in position not only by glue but also by the dowels and the mast tube. A single wooden dowel runs down through the funnel and then on through the cabin and hull, while two wooden dowels and the tube mast run through the

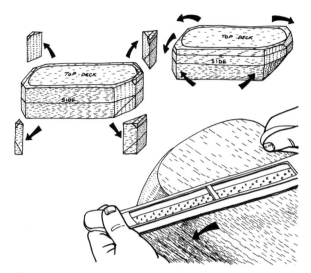

Illus. 5. Top left: Cut away the waste that can be seen from the top view. The widest bulge—the "belly" line, as seen in the side and end views—occurs 2" down from the top prow line. Top right and bottom: Use the rasp to reduce and shape the hull, working the wood to a smoothly curved finish.

cabin and into the hull. The dowel and the glue make for firm easy-to-make joints.

Take the 12"-long piece of 3"-wide, 1½"-thick pine and, allowing for end waste, cut it down into two pieces at 6" and 3¼". Shaping the cabin is easy enough; all you do is establish the "top" face and then rasp away the top edges and the corners until you have a nicely round-edged cabin that sits flat on the deck (Illus. 6, middle and bottom left). The funnel is a little more tricky in that the profile is more complex. Having established and labelled the various faces, rub the "bottom" face with sandpaper until the funnel sits true and square on top of the cabin. Trace off the side-view profile and pencil-press-transfer the traced lines through to the side of the wood. Make two straight cuts with the saw to remove the bulk of the waste. Now use the rasp to round off all the corners and edges (Illus. 6, middle-to-bottom right).

Once you have achieved two good shapes for the cabin and the funnel, rub them down with the graded sandpapers until they are completely smooth to the touch.

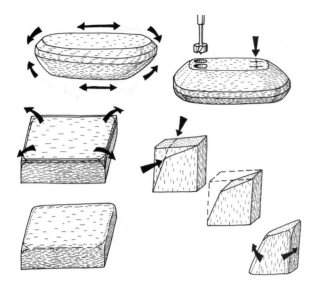

Illus. 6. Top left: With the graded sandpapers, remove the rough rasp texture and rub down to a smooth finish. Top right: Use the drill press and the 2½″-diameter Forstner bit to bore out the 1″-deep caster holes. Middle and bottom left: Shape the cabin with the rasp, rounding the top edges and corners. Middle-to-bottom right: Make two straight cuts to clear the waste from the funnel; then use the rasp and sandpaper to round off the shape.

Putting the Piece Together

When you have cut, shaped, and finished the three forms that make up the tugboat—the hull, cabin, and funnel—take a pencil, ruler, and square, and very carefully establish the position of the cabin on the deck and the funnel on the cabin. When you are satisfied with the fit, smear white PVA wood adhesive on all mating surfaces, place the cabin and the funnel in position, and put them to one side until the glue is set.

While the glue is drying, take another look at Illus. 3 and note how the three dowels, the mast tube, and the four stanchions are placed in relationship to each other. Bearing in mind that all the dowels, tubes, or stanchions are ¾″ in diameter, establish the position of the holes and carefully mark the hole-centers with a punch (Illus. 7, top left). Set the drill press

up with a long-shanked, ¾″-diameter bit and bore out all the holes. Being careful so that the bit doesn't wander or slip, run all the holes at least an inch deep into the hull.

Having made sure that the holes are free from dust and debris, use a pencil and a scrap of cardboard to establish the depth of the holes and the subsequent length of the dowels or tubes (Illus. 7, bottom right). Use a small saw or hacksaw to cut the items to length. Once you've cut them to length, take the dowels a piece at a time and pencil in the part to be glued; then drag that part of the dowel over a large-toothed saw so as to score the wood with a number of glue grooves (see Illus. 1 on page 16). Do this with all the wooden dowels.

When you come to gluing the dowels, rather than dribbling glue into the holes and risking the dowels being swamped and not settling correctly, it's much better to just smear glue on the sides and bottom of the dowels and tap them home. The same goes for fastening the mast tube and stanchions. Establish the in-

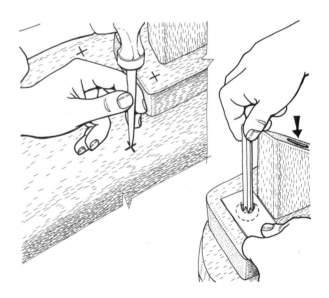

Illus 7. Top left: Establish the position of the various holes and carefully mark the hole-centers with a punch. Bottom right: Use a pencil and a scrap of cardboard to measure the depth of each hole and to establish the length of the dowels or tubes.

the-hole lengths, cut the two stanchion rails to length, swivel the stanchions so that you can slide the rails into place, and finally fit and secure with a small amount of two-tube resin glue.

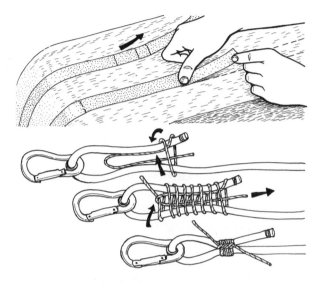

Illus. 8. Top: Spend time making sure that the taped curves are crisply set out and smoothed down onto the wood. Bottom: When you are ready to attach the pull-cord, first bind each end of the rope to prevent it from fraying. Loop the end through the clip and lay the twine between the loop. Pass the twine around and around the rope eight times; then thread the twine end through the initial loop and pull on both twine ends. Finally, knot and tie to secure.

Painting

Turn back to the project picture (Illus. 1) and the painting grid (Illus. 3, bottom), and see how the tugboat is painted and finished. The bottom part of the hull is blue, the middle area is left natural and varnished, and the top part and the deck are painted orange. Note the bright-red fender rings, the white cabin, the black portholes, the orange funnel, and all the other painted details.

When you have considered exactly how you want your tugboat to be painted, lightly pencil in the 2″-from-the-top prow line and establish the position of the red fender rings, the portholes, and the large circle on the top deck. Take the masking tape and, being sure to place it on the unpainted side of the line, establish the gently curved lines that delineate the edge of the orange area, the edge of the blue area, and so on. Spend time making sure that the taped curves are crisply set out and smoothed into position (Illus. 8, top). Having double-checked that all is correct, start the painting by applying the main blocks of color. Be careful not to have the paints so thick that they blob or so thin that they run. Paint up to the drawn lines and angles, and slightly over the lines that are set out with masking tape. When the paint is dry, ease away the masking tape, use a pair of compasses to set out the fenders, the large circle on the top deck, and the portholes, and then use a fine-point brush to block in the circles.

Once you have blocked in all the details and maybe even given the tug a name and number (perhaps a child's name and age), make sure that the acrylic paint is completely dry and give the whole workpiece a couple of well-brushed coats of clear yacht varnish.

Adding the Attachments

When the varnish is dry, then comes the really exciting part of fitting the boat out with all the hardware that makes this toy so special—the rubber fender strips, the casters or wheels, and the large screw-eyes.

Starting with the rubber fender strips, take a close look at your particular product and see how the screws need to be placed and the cover slid into position. Note: There are many types of fenders and methods of attaching them, so read all the literature beforehand. Cut the strips to length, establish precisely where they need to be placed, and draw in guidelines. Attach the fender strips with screws or clips, depending on which were supplied by the manufacturer.

Your particular casters or wheels will need to be attached according to the manufacturer's instructions. Some are simply attached with screws, while others have a single pivotal hole, and still others are secured with clips, and so on. The only thing to bear in mind, when you are attaching the casters or wheels, is that they should be free to swing and rotate without rubbing against some part of the hull. Thus, in some instances, you might need to bore out slightly larger-diameter holes, to cut away the sides of the holes with a gouge, or even to have the holes set deeper or possibly shallower.

When you come to attaching the screw-eyes, it's best to first mark the position of the screw and then to run a small drilled pilot hole $1/2''$ or so into the wood.

Finally, slide the rubber end-stop over the mast, loop and bind the rope to the shackle clips (Illus. 8, bottom), and the tugboat is ready for her maiden voyage around the playroom.

Hints and Modifications

- If you can obtain an $8 \times 6''$ section of wood, then you only need to buy a single 24''

length, and you will be able to forego the gluing-up stage.
- If you can't obtain a large section of wood, there's no reason why you shouldn't use, say, four glued-together $3 \times 3''$ sections and modify the design accordingly.
- The design of the tugboat is dependent on the availability and your selection of store-bought products—the color and design of the plastic or rubber fender strip, whether the tubing is made of copper, brass, or stainless-steel, and the shape of the casters or wheels. So, you might have to modify the design accordingly—the size of the tube, the colors to match the tube or the fenders, the depth of the caster holes, and so on.
- For increased maneuverability, you could redesign the arrangement of the casters or wheels, and have two wheels at the back and a single wheel at the front.
- If you are worried about damage to walls and furniture, you could use a complete wrap-around white plastic fender.
- If you decide to have a higher mast, more screw-eyes, or whatever, make sure that they are safely placed, nicely rounded, and buffered with rubber stops.

7

A PULL-ALONG NOAH'S ARK

*An Ark on wheels with flat animals and figures,
painted with traditional imagery*

*Primary techniques: scroll-saw work,
basic carving, chuck and center turning, and
freehand painting*

The Noah's Ark toy is a real beauty! With its high-pitched roof, traditionally painted flower-and-leaf dado, big fat wheels, and good supply of brightly painted animals and figures, it has all the characteristics of a classic pull-along toy for toddlers. Drawing inspiration from the German Arks painted with flowers that were made in Berchtesgaden in the 1830s and the beautifully naïve slab-based folk Arks that were made in and around Pennsylvania between 1810 and 1900, this toy is just asking to be played with.

What toddler will be able to resist the quiet playtime pleasures of flipping back the lid, setting the animals and figures out in rows, and then trundling the Ark across the unexplored oceans of the garden or playroom! And then again, what woodworking parent, grandparent, or friend will be able to resist fretting, carving, turning, and painting this marvellously elaborate project!

Design and Technique Considerations

Have a long leisurely look at the working drawings, diagrammatic cutting grid, painting grids, and step-by-step details, and see how the Ark, animals, and figures need to be worked, put together, and painted. Note, for

Illus. 1. Project picture.

example, how the slab that goes to make up the deck is cut and carved, how the wheels are turned, recessed, drilled, and mounted, how the figures are cut from plywood, how the motifs are transferred and painted, and so on.

Consider how this project offers a chance to broaden your skills in that it involves such exciting and diverse techniques as turning, scroll-saw work, carving, and freehand painting.

Study the details and consider the primary measurements. The Ark is about 16″ long from stem to stern, 10″ high, and 6″ wide. Note the way the roof swings up on four brass strap hinges, how the structure is butt-jointed and fastened with nails, how the wheels are

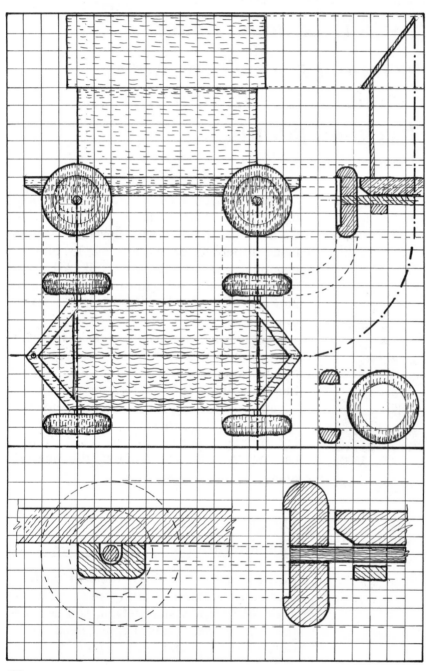

Illus. 2.   Working drawings. Top: The scale is one grid square to 1″. Bottom: The scale is two grid squares to 1″.

attached directly to the axles, and how the axles are contained by little U-shaped bearing blocks.

Spend time considering just how the project relates to your tools. Do you have a lathe? Do you have a scroll saw? Such points need to be carefully thought through. With that said, if you like the overall idea of the project but want to buy ready-made wheels, have the figures turned instead of cut from plywood, or change the project so as to avoid turning or whatever, then there's no problem; all you do is modify the designs accordingly. One of the pleasures of working a project like this is the fact that there is plenty of room for your own ideas.

Once you have a good clear understanding

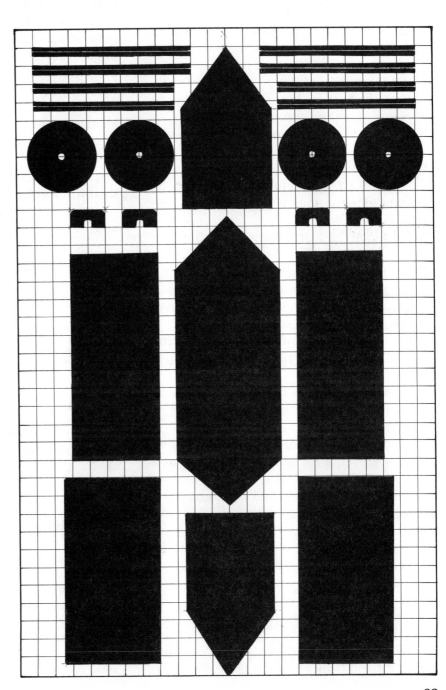

Illus. 3. Diagrammatic cutting grid. The scale is one grid square to 1".

of the tool and material implications of the project, draw the designs up to full size.

Tools and Materials

- A plank of prepared 1″-thick wood that is 17″ long and 7″ wide—for the base (this allows for wastage).
- A 6″-wide, 72″-long strip of best-quality, ¼″-thick multicore plywood—for the house.
- A 72″ length of ¼ × ¼″-square wood (or remnants of various sizes)—for strengthening the inside angles.
- A sheet of best-quality, ¾″-thick multicore plywood—for the figures and animals.
- A 24″ length of ⅜″- to ½″-diameter dowel—for the two axles.
- A 12″ length of 4¼ × 4¼″-square wood (it's best to use an easy-to-turn wood like beech or ash)—for the four wheels and the pull-ring.
- A 10″ length of 2 × 1″ wood—for the four axle brackets.
- Four small strap hinges with screws to fit, preferably made of brass—for the roof.
- A quantity of short slender nails with small heads.
- A yard of cord, preferably a soft, fat, cotton "yachting" rope—for the pull-rope.
- A pencil and ruler.
- The use of a workbench with a vise and hold-down.
- The use of a lathe.
- A good selection of turning tools, including a skew chisel, a round-nosed gouge, and a parting tool.
- A pair each of dividers and callipers.
- A scroll saw—we use a Hegner.
- A straight saw.
- A selection of wood-carving tools, including a small straight chisel, a V-section tool, and a U-section gouge.
- A small mallet.
- A good selection of acrylic paints.
- All the usual workshop items, such as a hammer, a screwdriver, brushes, PVA adhesive, a hand drill with a range of drill bits, a Surform rasp, a plane, a scalpel, and sandpaper.

Cutting and Carving the Boat-Shaped Base Slab

Having inspected your wood to make sure that it is free from such nasties as splits, dead knots, and stains, arrange your tools and materials so that they are close at hand and pin up your designs and drawings so that they are within view. Secure the 17″-long base slab best-face up on the workbench. Set it out with a center-line, and establish the shape of the stem, the stern, and the two sunken triangular areas: the pulpit at the stem and the cockpit at the stern. Note how the stem, or prow (you might call it the front end), is slightly sharper than the stern.

Having measured and marked in the length and shape of the boat slab, take the straight

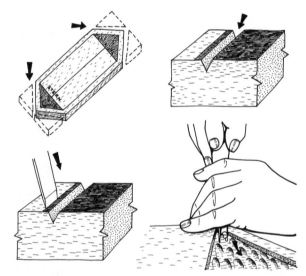

Illus. 4. Top left: Cut away the four small triangles of waste, set out the ¾″-wide border, and establish the position of the triangular sunken areas. Top right: Cut a V-section trench around the triangles. The trench needs to be ⅛″ to the waste side of the drawn line. Bottom left: Hold the tool so that it is angled slightly over the border margin. Bottom right: Using the V-section trench as a depth guide, work across the grain and remove the waste with small scooping strokes.

saw and cut away the four small triangular pieces of waste (Illus. 4, top left). Use the rasp and sandpaper to take the sawn angles to a smooth finish. Set out the ¾"-wide border that runs right around the shape of the deck, and then use the border to establish the shape and position of the triangular sunken areas. Label the "stern" end and shade in the areas that need to be lowered.

Secure the wood to the bench with the hold-down, and take the V-tool and cut a V-section trench around the triangles. Cut to the waste side and keep about ⅛" away from the drawn lines (Illus. 4, top right). Try to achieve a uniform depth of about ¼".

Once you have trenched around both triangles, take a small straight chisel and set in on the drawn line. Set the blade on the line, hold the tool so that the handle is angled slightly over the border margin, and set in around the triangles with a series of short sharp chops (Illus. 4, bottom left). As you set in, the small strip of waste between the drawn line and the V-trench will crumble away to reveal a crisp vertical face. Having set in both triangles, take the shallow-curve spoon gouge and clear away the waste to a depth of ¼". It's best to use the V-section trench as a depth guide and to work across or at an angle to the run of the grain (Illus. 4, bottom right). Don't try to remove the full depth of waste at a single stroke, but rather, lower the waste little by little. Aim, in this instance, to finish the wood with a chisel and to keep the lowered face smooth and free from tool marks.

When you have finished the deck, turn the slab over and use the plane to cut back the bevel on the underside edge. Then take the graded sandpapers and rub the whole workpiece down to a smooth finish.

Building the House

Study the working drawings in Illus. 2 and the diagrammatic cutting grid in Illus. 3, and note how the house is sized and placed so that the end gable walls are set back slightly from the edge of the lowered areas. See, also, how the long walls are set back from the deck edge by the width of the ¾" margin. Having carefully noted how the roof relates to the walls and the walls to the deck slab, use a pencil, measure, and square, and cut out the six plywood boards that go into making up the house. You need three pairs of boards in all: the two gable ends at 5" wide and 9" high, the two long walls at 10½" long and 5½" high, and the two roof boards at about 11½" long and 5" wide. It's best to cut the gable walls first and then to cut and adjust the other four boards to fit.

When you come to putting the walls together, start by gluing and nailing the gable walls onto the edges of the long walls. When you have made the four-wall shell, use the ¼ × ¼"-square wood to strengthen and square up the inside angles and to fit the house to the deck slab (Illus. 5, top right). Note that the strips inside the house will need to be cut and trimmed to fit.

Cut the two roof boards to size, and then chamfer and hinge the mating roof ridge edges

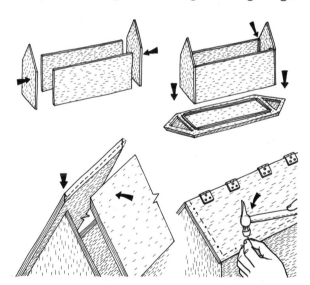

Illus. 5. Top left: Glue and nail the gables onto the edges of the long walls. Top right: Use the ¼ × ¼"-square wood to strengthen the walls and to fit the house to the deck slab. Bottom left: Chamfer the mating ridge edges so that the two boards close to a good tight fit. Bottom right: Carefully glue and nail one side of the roof.

so that the two boards close to a good tight fit against the gable (Illus. 5, bottom left).

Finally, dribble a small amount of glue on one slope of each gable end, carefully place the roof into position on the gable, and fasten with nails (Illus. 5, bottom right).

Turning the Wheels and the Pull-Ring

Having seen how there are five turnings—four wheels and a pull-along ring, all at 4″ in diameter—take your 12″ length of 4¼ × 4¼″-square wood and establish the end-centers by drawing crossed diagonals. Set the dividers to a radius of 2″, and scribe the ends of the wood out with 4″-diameter circles. Draw tangents at the diagonal-to-circle crossover points, and link up the resultant end-of-wood octagons so as to establish the corner waste. Use the plane to swiftly cut down the bulk of the waste.

Making sure that the lathe is in good condition, set the now-octagonal piece of wood in the jaws of the chuck, bring up the tailstock so that the wood is supported at both end-centers, and position the T-rest as close as possible to the work and just a fraction below lathe-center height. Check carefully through your pre-switch-on safety list (on page 17) and then switch on.

Start by using the round-nosed gouge to swiftly cut the wood down to a round section. Run the tool backward and forward along the wood until you achieve a smooth cylindrical section that is as close as possible to 4″ in diameter. When this is done, take another look at the various details and see how all the turnings are about 1¼″ thick and round-edged. See, also, how both the wheels and the pull-ring are set in and hollow-turned at a point about ¾″ from the circumference edge. The wheels have their centers lowered by about ¼″, while the pull-ring is pierced and shaped.

Having noted all the details, take the dividers and, allowing for about 1½″ of waste at the chuck and 1″ of waste at the tailstock, set the

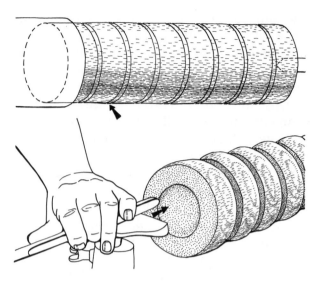

Illus. 6. Top: Set the wood off, from left to right, so that there are six 1¼″ step-offs between the waste wood at each end. Bottom: Lower the middle of the wheels to the ¼″ depth of the pilot cut.

wood off, from left to right, with alternating 1¼″- and ¼″-wide step-offs. Start and finish with a ¼″ step-off so that you have six 1¼″ step-offs in all. This allows for four wheels, one pull-ring, a spare wheel or ring, and parting off waste in between (Illus. 6, top). Having marked off the cylinder, use the parting tool to sink the waste between each wheel in to a depth of about an inch. Take the skew chisel and, working from the top-center and down into the between-wheel sinking, turn off the sharp shoulders at each side of the 1¼″-wide step-offs. Aim for a smooth half-circle nosing.

With the wood still held in the chuck, part off the end-of-cylinder waste, remove the tailstock, and set the tool rest over the bed of the lathe so that you can approach the wood end on. Take the round-nosed gouge and cut back the end-grain face. Work from side to center, until you reach the face of the first wheel.

Having turned the end of the wood down so that the flat face of the wheel runs in a smooth curve into the edge-of-wheel nosing, set the face of the disc out with the dividers so that it has a ¾″-wide "tire." Use the point of the skew chisel to sink a pilot cut in to a depth of about ¼". Still working from side to center, take a skew chisel or a round-nosed gouge and lower the whole middle-of-wheel area to the ¼" depth of the pilot cut (Illus. 6). Use the graded sandpapers to take the wheel to a good smooth finish, pencil in the center, and part the wheel off.

And so you continue, repeating the same procedure for the other wheels. When you come to the pull-ring, you run through all the procedures as described, except that when you come to sinking the middle-of-wheel recess, you don't stop short at a depth of ¼"; instead you run the recess straight through the thickness of the disc so as to make a ring.

Fitting the Wheels

Having turned the wheels and used the scroll saw to cut out the four little bridge-shaped U-bearings, study the details at the bottom of Illus. 2 and see how the wheels are glued to the ends of the axles, while at the same time

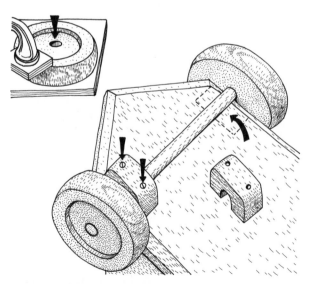

Illus. 7. Top left: Clamp the wheels face up on a scrap of wood and bore out the axle holes. Bottom: Align the axles so that they are square with the Ark and parallel to each other; then bridge the axles with the bearings and fasten with screws.

the axles are free moving but held secure by the U-bearings.

Measure the width of the Ark, allowing for the thickness of the wheels and a small space between the back of the wheels and the sides of the Ark, to give free movement; then cut the two dowel axles to length. Now take the drill and a bit to match the size of your dowel and bore out the centers of the wheels (Illus. 7, top left). Ideally, the wheels should be a tight push-fit on the ends of the axles. Note: A slot cut in the end of the axle will hold the glue and ensure a good tight bond.

Fit and glue the wheels on the axles. Drill screw holes through the U-bearings, align the axles so that they are square with the Ark and parallel with each other, and screw the bearings in place (Illus. 7, bottom). Note that the screws will need to be removed for painting. Finally, bore a pull-cord hole through the front of the prow.

Scroll-Sawing the Animal and Figure Profiles

Take a good look at the cutting-and-painting grids (Illus. 8–10), and note that the figures and animals are all cut from best-quality, birch-faced, ¾"-thick multicore plywood. Set your plywood out on the bench and check it over for possible problems. Ideally, it should be smooth, veneer-layered, and free from splits, warps, filler, knot holes, stains, and edge cavities.

Having noted how, at a grid scale of one square to ¼", Mr. and Mrs. Noah are about 4" high, while, say, the tiger is 4" long and the elephant is 2½" high, use a soft pencil to carefully trace off the profiles. Flip the tracing over so that it is face down, arrange it so as to avoid waste, secure it with tabs of masking tape, and then use a hard pencil to press-transfer the traced profile lines through to the wood. Trace off two profiles for each animal, and adjust the horns or whatever so as to have a male and a female. When this is done, remove the tracing

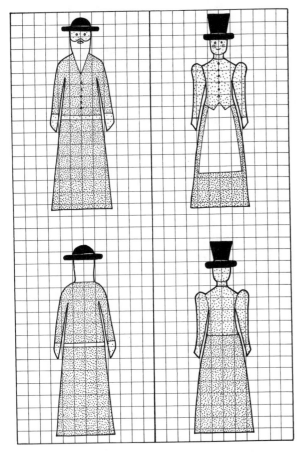

Illus. 8. Working drawings—Mr. and Mrs. Noah. Cutting-and-painting grid—the scale is one grid square to ¼".

paper and use a ball-point pen to establish a single clear cutting line.

Make sure that the scroll saw is in good condition, check through your pre-switch-on safety list (page 17), tension the saw blade, and switch on. Start by cutting the sheet down into manageable pieces. Take the animals and figures a piece at a time, hold them firmly down on the cutting table, and run them into the scroll-saw blade. Work at an easy steady pace, all the while turning and maneuvering the wood so that the blade is always presented with the line of the next cut (Illus. 11, top left). When you come to a tight angle, mark time with the wood so that the saw cuts broaden at the point of the angle, and then change the direction of the cut. Be warned: If you try to

run in and out of an angle, all in the same movement, then the chances are you will twist and break the saw blade. It's always a good idea to have a stack of spare blades!

When you have cut out the figures and animals, give them a swift rubbing down with a fine-grade sandpaper so as to remove all the sharp burrs and edges. Aim to leave all the edges looking slightly rounded (Illus. 11, bottom right).

Painting and Finishing

With the Ark, figures, and animals all rubbed down to a smooth finish, spend time looking at the working drawings and painting grids. The Ark imagery—the shape, form, and color

Illus. 9. Working drawings—animals. Cutting-and-painting grid—the scale is one grid square to ¼".

of the motifs—draws its inspiration from Arks that were made in Germany in the early nineteenth century. Such Arks are characterized by the wavy roof-tile design, the broad band of flowers and leaves that runs just under the eaves, and the stone design of the windows, door portico, and quoins (Illus. 12). The figures, on the other hand, resemble the figures that were made in the late nineteenth century in the Erzgebirge mountains (Illus. 8), while the animals draw their inspiration from certain modern designs (Illus. 9 and 10). All in all, we have opted for imagery that is full of authentic detail and interest.

Noting that the roof is two shades of brown, the walls are a bluish off-white, the stone

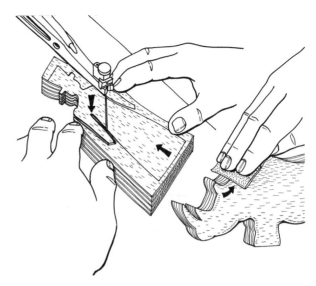

Illus. 11. Top left: When you come to using the scroll saw, mark time at tight angles so that the blade has a chance to broaden the cut and change direction. Bottom right: Use the fine-grade sandpaper to remove any burrs, and aim to leave the edges smooth and slightly rounded.

Illus. 10. Working drawings—more animals. Cutting-and-painting grid—the scale is one grid square to ¼".

details are two shades of grey, the band of flowers is red, dark-green, and white on a light-green ground, the boat slab is a rich brown, and the wheels are red, set out all your paints and brushes and generally prepare your working area for painting. Prior to painting, unscrew the bearing blocks so that the Ark and the wheel axles can be painted as separate items, push thumbtacks into the bottom of the figures and animals so as to prevent the painted items from coming into contact with the bench, and suspend the wheel axles and pull-ring from a line.

Start by giving the whole project—the Ark, the wheel axles, the pull-ring, and the figures and animals—a couple of coats of white primer. Apply the paint in thin coats, making sure that you avoid build-up on sharp angles and corners. Rub down between coats. When the second coat is completely dry, also rub down all runs and blobs. When this is done, apply all the main ground colors: light brown for the roof, a rich light green for the pattern strip under the eaves, off-white for the walls, dark brown for the hull and all the ground colors for the animals. Note: Some animals, such as the swans, zebras, and geese, are best left with the white undercoat as the ground color.

While the paint is drying, cut the tracings to fit the various sides of the Ark as well as the back and front faces of the animals and figures. With the tracings well placed, secure them with tabs of masking tape. Take a ball-point pen and carefully press-transfer the lines of the design through to the wood.

Note: If you consider the designs complicated, then it might be a good idea to do the tracings and painting in stages. In stage one, you would paint the ground color; in stage two, you would pencil-press-transfer the large

Illus. 13. Painting the animals. Top left: Pencil-press-transfer the secondary details through to the undercoated surface. Top right: Stand the animal on drawing pins to keep it off the work surface, and paint the secondary colors. Bottom left: Use a darker color on an almost dry brush to create the shaggy texture, and darken the "shaded" areas of the leg. Bottom right: Press-transfer the final details through to the animal, and use a darker color and a fine-point brush to bring out the details.

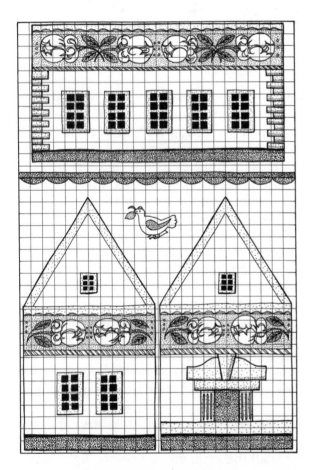

Illus. 12. Working-drawing painting grid. The scale is approximately two grid squares to 1″.

areas of color; in stage three, you would paint the large blocks of color; in stage four, you would pencil-press-transfer the fine details; and so on.

Remove the tracings and if necessary go over the transferred lines with a pencil to make sure that they are crisp and well established. When you are ready for painting, take your selected acrylic colors and a fine-point brush, and block in the areas of secondary color on the Ark, figures, and animals (Illus. 13). Animals such as the camel, monkey, male lion, and moose need to be textured so that they look shaggy. This is best achieved by using a fine brush loaded with almost-dry paint. Stroke the brush in the direction of the "hair." When you come to painting the Ark and the figures, you might accentuate the scoops of the roof tiles with a slightly darker shade of brown, paint the main body of the flower petals white, paint Mr. Noah's cloak green, Mrs. Noah's skirt red, her jacket blue, their hats black, the stonework grey, the fea-

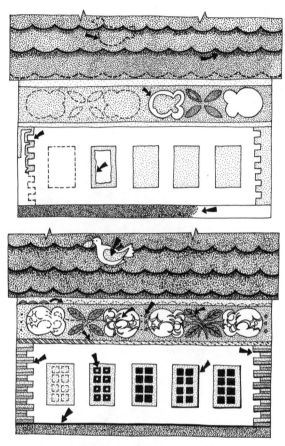

Illus. 14. Painting the Ark. Top: Having first painted in the main areas of color—the brown roof, the white walls, the brown base, and the green, red, and white border design—use the tracing to draw in the secondary details of the design. Use a fine-point brush to highlight the scoop of the roof tiles, the white roses, the green leaves, and the grey stonework. Bottom: Pencil-press-transfer the final details through to the painted surface. Paint the bird white and blue, add a little touch of pink to the roses and borders, add a dark-green line to the leaves and stems, accentuate the dark-grey "shadow" on the stonework, and finally use black to bring out the details of the windows and stonework.

ture details of the figures and the lines around the window frames black, and so on. As you continue working, gradually paint smaller and smaller details, one color upon another, until you are satisfied with the overall effect (Illus. 14). When the paint is completely dry, sign the underside of the Ark with the date and apply a couple of generous coats of clear yacht varnish on all surfaces. Finally, reattach the wheel axles and bearing blocks, remove the thumbtacks, knot a good length of cord to the Ark and the pull-ring, and the project is done.

Hints and Modifications

- Instead of having the hinges show, you can attach them on the underside. Either way, you need to cut the roof mitre and attach the hinges so that the roof flap can be folded right back.
- You could modify the deck slab by building it up from layers of plywood, or you could have a smooth deck with an added beading.
- If you don't have the use of a lathe, you could use the scroll saw to cut the wheels from flat stock or buy some wheels ready-made.
- For the figures and animals to stand upright, the base edges need to be cut smooth and square.
- If you decide to make all the figures—Mr. and Mrs. Noah, their three sons, and their three sons' wives—then make the sons shorter and beardless and the daughters-in-law shorter and dressed in different colored clothes.
- Making male and female pairs of animals usually means changing small details, such as leaving off the horns for the female, adding a shaggy mane for the male, giving the female a pouch, and so on.
- If you want to make other Ark toys, you might want to look at our book *Making Noah's Ark Toys in Wood*, also published by Sterling.

8
A PULL-ALONG SAUSAGE DOG

A dachshund with ball-wheels and body movement

Primary techniques: shaping, drilling, fretting, laminating, assembling, and staining

Most children enjoy playing with dogs. Poodles, terriers, collies, and hounds ... small, large, smooth, and shaggy—they are all good fun. I think most of us like dogs because we see something of ourselves in their various forms and personalities.

One of my favorite breeds is the dachshund, or sausage dog. With their long bodies, sleek smooth coats, short legs, and bright sparkling intelligent eyes, dachshunds make wonderful pets. Okay, so sausage dogs aren't so hot when it comes to running, fighting, and fetching, but they sure know how to project their personality and have a good time. And then again, it has to be said that there is something very funny about a dog that is so long and short-legged that when it walks, its belly almost bounces on the ground.

So, if you are looking to make a toy with lots of charm and personality, a toy with unique movement, you can't do better than this friendly, wibbly-wobbly, curvy-swirvy pull-along sausage dog!

Design and Technique Considerations

Take a look at the working drawings (Illus. 2 and 3) and see how the dachshund, just like a string of sausages, is made up of a number of nearly identical sausage-shaped units. Note, also, the way the units are linked together by a 1½"-wide leather strap that runs

Illus. 1. Project picture.

from the dog's head, through the body of the dog, to become the tail. Each of the identical body units is 2" long, 1⅝" wide, and 1½" high, with a loose, centrally placed through-body axle and a pair of shop-bought bead ball-wheels. With that said, note that the head unit is longer than the body units. Consider how the dog can be as short as three units—a tail, a head, and a single body sausage—or as long as you like—with a head and a tail and as many sausage units as you care to make in between. Our dog is made up of five sections: a head unit, a tail unit, and three body units. If you want to make a really long sausage dog, then all you do is replicate the number of 2″-long body units.

Having seen how the strap runs through the body to link and hinge the units, study the top detail of Illus. 3 and note how the head is made up of seven ⅛″-thick plywood cutouts that are laminated together to make a single ⅞″ thickness. About halfway along the front unit, the

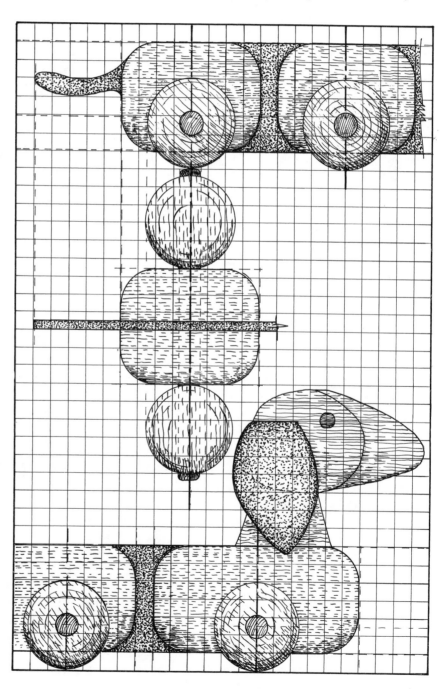

Illus. 2. Working drawings. The scale is four grid squares to 1″.

$\frac{1}{8}$"-thick leather strap stops short to be butted up against the $\frac{1}{8}$"-thick plywood tenon that helps hold the head to the body.

The sausage dog is a good project for beginners, in that, apart from a small amount of fretwork and shaping, it can be put together from ready-made off-the-shelf materials: large wooden beads for the wheels, a thick leather belt or strap, dowel, prepared timber sections, a miniature dog collar, and a dog leash.

Tools and Materials

- A 24″ length of prepared $1\frac{1}{2} \times \frac{3}{4}$″ wood—this makes a five-unit dog that is 13 to 15″ long from nose to tail, and allows for wastage.
- A 24″-long, $1\frac{1}{2}$″-wide, $\frac{1}{8}$″-thick leather strip or strap—it's best if it's dark brown and unpolished on both sides.
- A sheet of $\frac{1}{8}$″-thick, best-quality, birch-faced multicore plywood at about 12×12″—this allows for a small amount of waste.
- Ten large wooden beads at about $1\frac{1}{4}$″ in diameter—select a bright color like red.
- A 36″ length of $\frac{1}{4}$″-diameter dowel—this allows for wastage.
- A quantity of white PVA glue.
- A craft knife and cutting board.
- A pencil and ruler.
- A try square.
- A small plane.
- A small rasp.
- A roll of double-sided transparent tape.
- A roll of masking tape.
- A small flat-bladed saw.
- A fretsaw or piercing saw with a pack of spare blades.
- The use of a bird's mouth fretsaw board with bench clamps to fit.
- The use of a drill press with bits at $\frac{1}{8}$″, $\frac{1}{4}$″, and $\frac{3}{8}$″.
- A pack of graded sandpapers.
- Acrylic paints in light brown and black.
- A couple of brushes: one broad and the other for fine details.

- A can of clear beeswax polish.
- A dog collar with a dog leash to match for a miniature type of dog.

Preparing the Wood and Shaping the Body Sections

When you have studied the designs, decided how long the dog is going to be, and purchased all your materials, take your length of prepared $1\frac{1}{2} \times \frac{3}{4}$″ wood and, with a pencil, label the wide faces "side" and "leather," and the narrow faces "top" and "bottom." On the "side" face, draw in a center-line that runs the length of the wood. Now, having first noted how the top-side and bottom-side edges need to be rounded, set the wood in the jaws of the vise and use the small plane to cut away the edge waste (Illus. 4, top). Work backward and forward along the wood, until you have cut the right angles down to a smooth part-circle curve. Having achieved a part-circle radius of about $\frac{1}{2}$″, use the graded sandpapers to rub the wood down to a smooth finish.

When you have shaped the wood along its entire length, use the small saw to cut it down into two 12″ lengths. Stick a strip of double-sided transparent tape down on one of the marked "leather" faces, and then set the two flat faces together so that all edges and angles are aligned. With the two lengths of wood sandwiched nicely together, take a pencil, ruler, and square, and set the wood off along its length with four step-offs at 2″ and a single step-off at 3″. The 12″ allow for a small amount of end and saw-kerf waste. When this is done, locate the center-point of each unit by using the square to run center-lines around the wood. Using the crossed center-lines as alignment guides, mark in the center of the axle pivot holes (Illus. 4, bottom). The hole-centers should be set on the vertical center-line at a point $\frac{3}{8}$″ down from the center of the unit. Note: If your beads are smaller than $1\frac{1}{4}$″ in diameter, you will have to set the holes farther down towards the base line. Mark all five axle

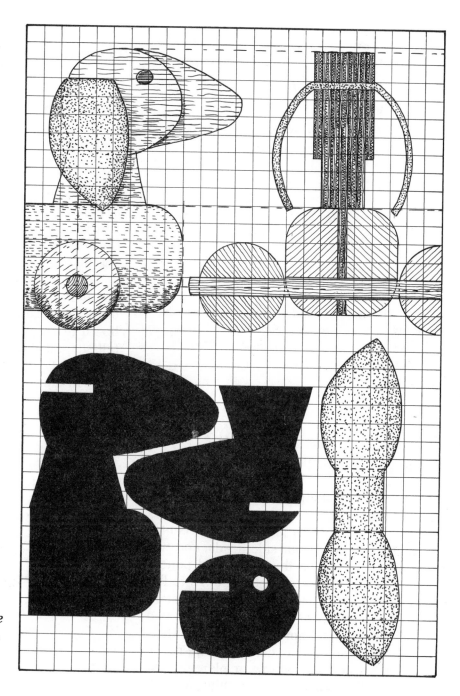

Illus. 3. Working drawings. The scale is four grid squares to 1″. Note the head, face, and ear profiles.

centers, double-check that all is correct, and then use the drill and ³⁄₈″-diameter bit to run holes through the double-thickness sandwich. Make sure that the drill is set at right angles to the working face of the wood so that entry and exit holes occur at the same point on the center-line.

When you have drilled out the five holes through the body—one through each marked-out step-off—use the straight saw to cut the wood down into the five separate units. Number both halves of the five matched pairs, with the head unit being number 1 and the tail unit being number 5. Finally, use the rasp and the graded sandpapers to rub the sawn side faces down to a smooth curve.

95

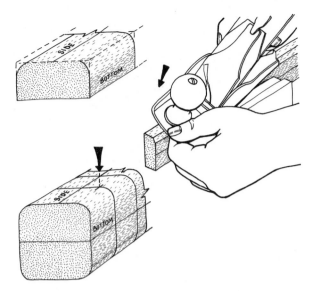

Illus. 4. Top: Set the wood in the vise and use the small plane to cut away the edge waste. Bottom left: Use the crossed lines as a guide to mark in the axle pivot holes.

Setting Out and Making the Plywood "Head" Laminates

Having carefully studied Illus. 3 and seen how the head is made up from seven separate ⅛"-thick plywood layers or laminates—one center through-body head, four side heads, and two side cheeks—trace off the profile and pencil-press-transfer the traced lines through to the working face of the multicore plywood. Establish the position of the eyes on the two "cheek" pieces and bore them out with the ⅛" drill bit. When this is done, use the bird's mouth table and the fretsaw or piercing saw to cut out the plywood profiles (Illus. 5, top). Bear in mind, when you are sawing, that, ideally, the blade should pass through the wood at right angles to the working face, and the line of cut should run a little to the waste side of the drawn line. Work at a steady even pace, trying all the while to maneuver the wood so that the saw is presented with the line of the next cut, and to regulate the speed of the saw stroke so as not to rip or tear the face of the

wood. When you have made the seven cutouts, rub them down with the graded sandpapers so as to remove all splinters and jags.

Fitting the Leather

Look back at Illus. 2 and see how the leather strap runs out through the tail end of the toy to become the tail. Allowing for about 1½" for the tail, separate the two halves of unit number 5, remove the double-sided transparent tape, and use one half to establish on the leather the shape and position of the tail. It's best to set the half-unit flat-face down on the leather and then to draw around it with a pencil. When you have drawn out on the leather the shape of the tail, use the craft knife and the cutting board to carefully cut out the little upturned tail shape (Illus. 5, bottom). Now, bearing in mind that the leather runs from the tail, through units 5, 4, 3, and 2, and then on half-way through unit number 1, where it butts up against the ⅛"-thick center-of-head plywood

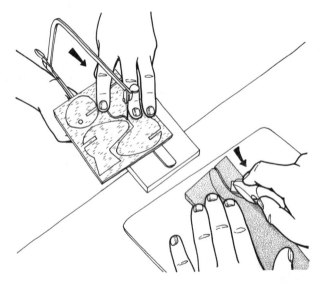

Illus. 5. Top: Use the bird's mouth table and the piercing saw to cut out the plywood head profiles. Bottom: Working on the cutting board, use the craft knife to cut out the tail shape at one end of the leather strip. Keep the leather moving so that the knife is always presented with the line of the next cut.

cutout, and also remembering that there needs to be a ¼″ gap between each unit, glue one half of the sausage dog in place on the leather strip, temporarily hold it in place with strips of masking tape, and glue the central plywood cutout in place on the half-unit number 1 (Illus. 6, top).

When the glue is dry, flip the half-dog over so that it is leather-or-ply-side down, support the leather on a strip of waste, and then take the drill and the ⅜″-diameter bit and run the axle holes on through the leather (Illus. 6, bottom). Now, with lengths of scrap dowel passed through each axle hole, smear glue over the other half-units and then slide them in place on the dowels. Having made sure that the units are matched up with their numbered other halves and aligned both with each other and the axle holes, bind up with masking tape. Wait a while for the glue to dry and then remove the tape and very carefully ease the lengths of scrap dowel out of their holes.

Assembling, Painting, and Finishing

When the glue is dry, make sure that the axle holes are free from bits of leather and blobs of dry glue. If necessary, run the ⅜″-diameter drill bit through each of the axle holes. Look back at the working-drawing details and see how the six remaining plywood "head" cutouts need to be set—three on each side of the central through-body cutout. Smear a small amount of glue on all mating faces and edges, and set the cutouts in position (Illus. 7, left). Making sure that there is a good amount of glue between the bottom edges of the plywood and the top face of the body unit, bind them together with strips of masking tape. When the glue is dry, remove the tape and rub down with the graded sandpapers what is now a ⅞″-thick head. Aim to round over the various steps that make up the profile (Illus. 7, right). Now slide the leather ear piece into the through-head slot and glue it into position.

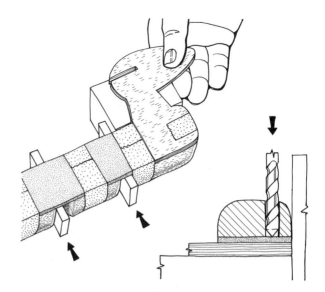

Illus. 6. Top: Glue the leather and central plywood head shape onto the half-units, using scraps of wood to support the leather and clamping up with straps of masking tape. Bottom: Run the ⅜″-diameter axle holes through the wood and leather and into the waste wood.

Clear away all the dust and debris, and move the workpiece to the area that you have set aside for painting. Mix the black and light-

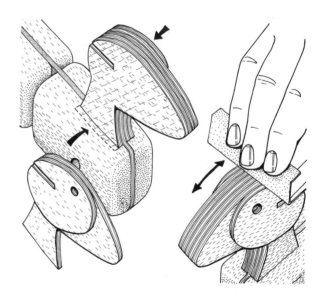

Illus. 7. Left: Glue all the mating faces and edges, and set the cutouts in position. Right: Use the graded sandpapers to rub the edges down to a smooth rounded finish.

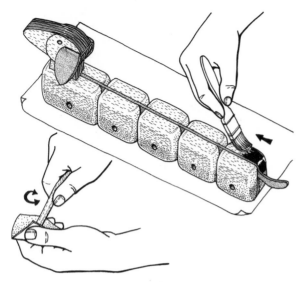

Illus. 8. Top: Put the partially made dog on newspaper and paint the top half of the dog black, being careful not to paint the leather. Bottom left: Round off the axle ends by rotating the dowel on the sandpaper.

brown acrylic paints to a thin wash and block in the areas that make up the design. Don't try for naturalistic realism; just settle for painting the belly of each unit light brown and the top half black (Illus. 8, top). Be careful not to get paint on the leather. Aside from the eyes, which are painted black, leave the head unpainted. When the paint is dry, give all surfaces a very light sanding. Then take the wax polish and the cloth and burnish the whole

toy to a dull sheen finish. Cut the ¼"-diameter axle dowels to length, round over the ends with a scrap of sandpaper (Illus. 8, bottom left), slide the dowel through the axle holes, and glue the ball-wheel beads in position. Allow for about 1/16" between moving surfaces.

Finally, fit the little dog collar in place around the dog's neck, clip on the leash, and the dachshund is ready for his first walk around the playroom.

Hints and Modifications

- When you are choosing your wood, select a type that is smooth-grained and free from knots. A dark, easy-to-work timber like mahogany is a good choice.
- If you decide to use more standard wheels, rather than the ball-wheels called for in the project, make sure that they are wide-rimmed and have washers.
- Make sure that your glue works well on leather and wood; do a test on a small scrap of leather.
- It's important for the axles to be a loose fit through the body and a tight fit in the beads. If you do have to ease the through-bead holes, be careful not to split the wood.
- If you decide to use varnish rather than wax, make sure that you don't get varnish on the leather.

9
A PULL-ALONG RABBIT ON A CYCLE

A rabbit with wheel-driven leg movement

Primary techniques: scroll sawing, drilling, painting, and assembling

Illus. 1. Project picture.

A good many of us have, at some time or other, either kept rabbits as pets or at least owned a toy rabbit. For most children, the very word "rabbit" brings to mind cuddly fluffy creatures with big floppy ears and white pom-pom tails, hopping and leaping about, chomping on carrots. This special affinity between children and rabbits is borne out by the numerous nicknames for rabbits and the many films, car-

toons, and stories in which they are featured. Think of cottontails, thumpers, hoppities, and bunnies . . . *Watership Down*, Bugs Bunny, and Brer Rabbit.

Our cycling road-racing rabbit may come across as a bit disdainful and haughty. Still, he is a real funny honey-bunny, who is just waiting to have his cord pulled and be put through his pumping-iron workout.

Design and Technique Considerations

Study the working drawings (Illus. 2 and 3) and the diagrammatic cutting grid (Illus. 4), and see how, at a grid scale of four squares to 1″, the toy stands about 6″ high and 6″ long, with a wheel span of a little less than 4″. Note the way the toy is made from two different thicknesses of plywood: 1″ for the back wheels and the main central bunny-and-bike through-body, and ¼″ for the front wheels, legs, and spacers. Of course, you could build the toy completely out of ¼″-thick material, making up the 1″ thickness by laminating four ¼″ layers, but using two different thicknesses is much easier.

Consider the way the various moving parts need to be spaced and distanced by plywood and brass washers. So, for example, at the back of the cycle, across the span of the thick back wheels, the attachment order from side to side is wheel, washer, spacer, washer, cycle body, washer, spacer, washer, and finally the other wheel. The same goes for across the span of the rabbit's hips. The attachment order is round-head screw, washer, upper leg, spacer, washer, spacer, cycle body, and the reverse order for the other side of the body. The spacers ensure that the various plywood layers are distanced from and stay parallel to one another, and the brass washers make for less friction. Note the way the legs are set with one up and one down, with the feet being pivoted with one at 12 o'clock and the other at 6

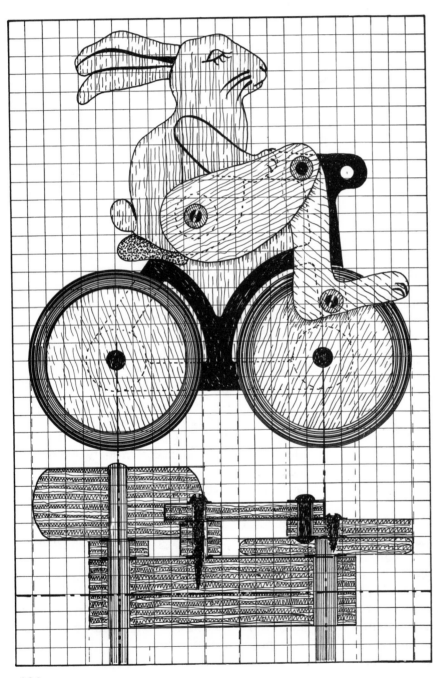

Illus. 2. Working drawings. The scale is four grid squares to 1".

o'clock. Such an arrangement creates a realistic cranklike pedalling movement.

As for the painting, only the frame, the feature details on the rabbit, and the saddle are painted—use black for the frame and details, and red for the saddle—while the whole toy is varnished. Note how the tire effect is created by rounding the wheel edges so as to reveal the veneer layers of plywood.

Tools and Materials

- Two 9 × 6″ sheets of best-quality, birch-faced multicore plywood: ¼″ and 1″.
- A sheet each of work-out and tracing paper.
- A pencil, ruler, compass, and square.
- The use of a drill press, with drill bits at ⅛″, ³/₁₆″, ¼″, and ⅜″.
- The use of an electric scroll saw—we use a Hegner.
- Four brass round-head or dome-head screws—two at 1¼″ and two at ½″—with 14 brass washers to fit.
- Two solid dome-head rivets—to pass through two sheets of ¼″ ply and three washers—with a tool set or anvil to fit.
- A small hammer.
- A 6″ length of ¼″ dowel with eight brass washers to fit.
- A small saw.
- A tube of Super Glue.
- A couple of yards of string or twine and a pack of large wire paper clips—for the drying line.
- Acrylic paints in black and red.
- A small can of clear varnish.
- A couple of brushes: a broad and a fine-point.
- A pack of graded sandpapers.
- A 36″ length of soft red cord—for the pull-cord.

Setting Out the Design, Drilling, and Scroll Sawing

When you have studied the working drawings (Illus. 2 and 3) and have a clear understanding of how the toy needs to be made and put together, set out all your tools and materials so that they are comfortably close at hand. Now, having checked that the plywood is in good condition, trace off the profiles that go into making up the design on the diagrammatic cutting grid (Illus. 4), and then pencil-press-transfer the traced images through to the working face of the plywood. The main body of the toy and the two back wheels need to be on the 1″-thick ply, and the two front wheels and all the other components on the ¼″-thick ply. Use a compass to mark in on the wheel the width of the round-edged tires. Make sure that the lines are clear and all the hole-centers are correctly placed.

When you have established the precise position of the hole-centers, mark each hole with the appropriate drill size. For example, the two through-cycle axle holes are ⅜″, the hip and foot holes ³/₁₆″, the through-wheel holes ¼″, and so on. When this is done, slide a sheet of waste wood under the wood to be drilled, and then set to work with the drill press, boring out the holes to the correct diameters (Illus. 5, top).

With all the holes bored out, take the wood to the scroll saw and start to fret out the various profiles. Using the saw is easy enough, as long as you work a little to the waste side of the drawn line, and as long as the blade is correctly tensioned and the table set so that the cut runs through the sheet of wood at right angles to the working face. Work at an easy controlled pace, all the while holding, steadying, and maneuvering the wood so that the blade is presented with the line of the next cut (Illus. 5, bottom).

Once you have fretted out all the profiles, pair up the various wheels and limbs, and then identify with a pencil mark the best face of each cutout. For instance, if one side of a wheel is in any way better than the other, then mark it so that it will be on show.

Rubbing Down, Painting, and Varnishing

Having fretted, drilled, and otherwise prepared all the plywood components, take the graded sandpapers and start the rubbing down. The washers, cycle-body, and limbs are easy enough—all you do is rub them down to a smooth, slightly round-edged finish—but the wheels are a little more tricky. If you look at Illus. 2, you will see that all the wheels, back and front, need to be worked to a fully round-edged, veneer-exposing finish. It's best to first run around the sawn edges of the wheels with the rasp, removing the sharp edges, and then

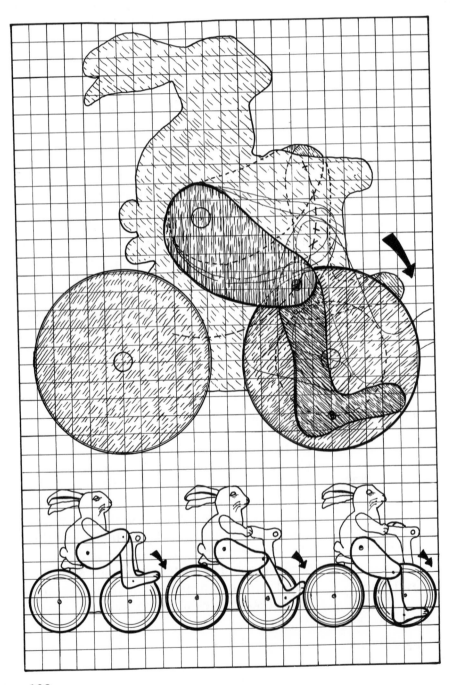

Illus. 3. Working drawings. The scale is four grid squares to 1". Note that the movement sequence at the bottom is not to scale.

to gradually sculpt the edges (Illus. 6, top) until they are rounded, and you have cut back to the compass-drawn line that marks out the edge of the tire rim (Illus. 6, bottom left). It's easy enough as long as you work with a gentle, rhythmic, controlled stroke of the rasp, all the while keeping the workpiece firmly clamped but rotating evenly while you are working.

When you have achieved a good round-edged shape with the rasp, rub down with the graded sandpapers. Continue until the exposed layers of ply are nicely curved and smooth (Illus. 6, bottom right). Work all faces, sawn edges, and holes to a smooth finish.

When all the components are ready to be painted, wipe them over so that they are free

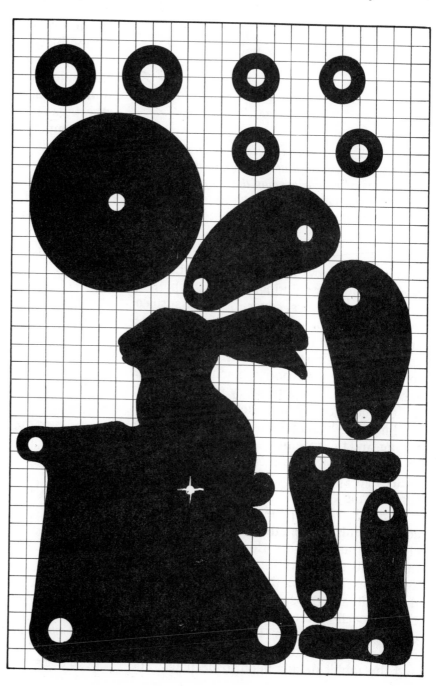

Illus. 4. Diagrammatic cutting grid. The scale is four grid squares to 1".

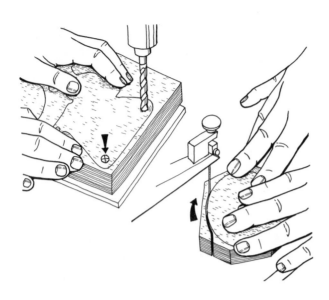

Illus. 5. Top: Slide a sheet of waste wood under the work to be drilled. Bottom: Work to the waste side of the drawn line, keeping the wood moving so that the saw blade is always presented with the line of the next cut.

from dust and move them to the area that you have set aside for painting. Set out the paints, varnish, and brushes, cover the work surface with newspaper, and rig up the twine-and-wire drying line. Knot the twine every 2 to 4″ along its length, and reshape the wire paper clips so as to make little hooks. Each component needs a hook. Have a trial dry run, arranging the cutouts side by side along the length of the line. The knots will keep the hooks from sliding, and the spacing between hooks should be such that the painted components can swing and spin without touching each other (Illus. 7, top).

Start by giving all the components a swift coat of varnish. When the varnish is dry, pencil-press-transfer the various design features through to the wood: the eyes, mouth, whiskers, arms, and paws through to each side of the rabbit, and the saddle, frame, and handle bars to each side of the cycle. When this is done, take the fine-point brush and the acrylic colors and paint in the design. The cycle frame and the rabbit details need to be black, and

the saddle should be red (Illus. 7, bottom). Paint both sides of the toy.

When the paint is completely dry, give all the components another well-brushed dribble-free coat of varnish and leave them to dry.

Putting the Piece Together and Finishing

When the varnish is dry, then comes the rather finger-twisting, knuckle-knotting task of putting the toy together. First, check that all the drilled holes are clean and free from paint and varnish. Take another look at the working drawings (Illus. 2 and 3), and then set out all the components, washers, screws, spacers, rivets, and dowels so that they are in an ordered arrangement across the work surface. Take a good look at the rivets, and see how your particular rivet type needs to be fitted, attached, and clenched.

Take the components to be riveted, the legs, and pair them up so that you have two mirror-

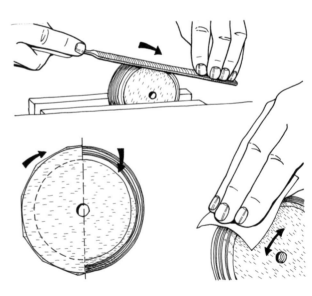

Illus. 6. Top: Secure the wheel in the vise and use the rasp to work the round-edged profile. Bottom left: First remove jagged-cut edges; then cut back to the compass-drawn line that marks the edge rim. Bottom right: Use the graded sandpapers to rub the wood down to a smooth round-edged shape.

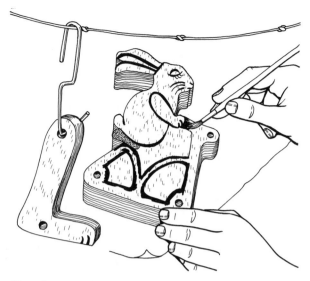

Illus. 7. Top: Knot the twine every 2 to 4″ along its length and reshape the paper clips so as to make hooks. Bottom: Use a fine-point brush to paint in the details of the rabbit and cycle; don't forget the rabbit's toes.

image legs that are placed so that the upper part of the leg laps over the lower. Now, one leg at a time, layer up the knee joint in the order of washer, ply, washer, ply, and washer, and slide the rivet through the joint so that the tail of the rivet comes through on the outside of the knee. When this is done, support the head of the rivet on the little anvil, and then use the hammer and the other half of the rivet set to tap over, shape, and finally clench the rivet. The knee joint needs to be riveted so that there is as little side-to-side skewing or twisting movement as possible, while still being easy and loose. Rivet both knees.

With the knee joints nicely pivoted, take the two front wheels, two washers, and a 1½″ length of ¼″ dowel, and set them in place on the front of the cycle. The attachment order from side to side is wheel, washer, cycle-body, washer, and wheel (Illus. 8). The wheels need to be an easy loose-turning fit through the cycle, with the ends of the dowel axles being glued into the wheel and cut flush. Have a trial dry-run fitting to get everything just right, and then fit and attach with Super Glue. Note: Once this type of glue has set, then it's set for good,

so be sure to get it right the first time. Attach the back wheels in like manner.

When the front wheels are in place, use the brass round-head screws to keep the upper legs in place at either side of the toy. One leg at a time, set two plywood spacers between the thigh pivot point and the rabbit's body, slide brass washers between the screw heads and between all ply layers, and then carefully screw the legs in place (Illus. 9). If the legs are correctly placed, the screw points should almost meet in the center of the 1″-thick plywood body. With the top of the legs pivoted on the rabbit's body, screw the feet at each side of the front wheels, so that the pivot points are about ¾″ out from the center of the wheel, and one foot is secured at 12 o'clock high and the other at 6 o'clock low. Don't forget about the washers between the screw heads and between the foot and the wheel.

Finally, when, by careful adjustment and fitting, you have achieved a smooth-running toy, loop the pull-cord and tie it onto the front of the cycle, and the rabbit is ready for his first race around the playroom.

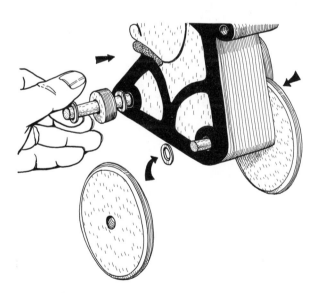

Illus. 8. Putting on the wheels. The order for the front wheels is wheel, washer, cycle, washer, and wheel. The order for the back wheels is wheel, washer, spacer, washer, cycle, washer, spacer, washer, and wheel.

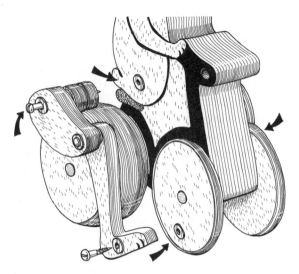

Illus. 9. Attaching the legs. The top-of-leg screw passes through a washer, the leg, a washer, a spacer, a washer, a spacer, another washer, and then into the body. The foot screw passes through the foot washer and into the wheel. Note that one foot is set at 12 o'clock high, while the other is set at 6 o'clock low.

Hints and Modifications

- With a toy of this character, it's important for the various moving parts to be able to slide smoothly and freely, one in front of another. Therefore, you might have to add additional brass washers between layers and/or rub down particular surfaces for a good fit. A little wax polish rubbed over the dry varnish creates a smooth friction-free surface.

- Rivets come in many shapes, sizes, and types, and most of them need to be clenched with a special tool or anvil. Ideally, you need a flat-headed, low-profile rivet. If you have any doubts as to the best rivet for the job, ask a specialist supplier for advice.

- If you like the overall idea of the toy but consider making the wheels a bit of a chore, you could consider using shop-bought wheels of different thicknesses and modifying the design accordingly.

- If you enjoy lathe work, you could turn plywood wheels between centers rather than fret them out on the scroll saw. Round discs of ply are cut out, pivoted between lathe centers, and then edge-turned, like miniature dishes.

- If you have a band saw, you could set up a circle-cutting jig and cut the wheels out of plywood.

10
A PULL-ALONG AIRPLANE

A biplane with a flick-around propeller and a pilot

Primary techniques: turning, fretting, whittling, assembling, and painting

This 1918 Handley Page biplane will inspire all manner of play that has to do with pioneer flying. When the daredevil pilot is popped into his cockpit, the giant propeller flicked round, and the big fat wheels set rolling, the won-derful flying machine will be ready to roar and *bbrooom* into action.

With its yesteryear details and turned, carved, cut, and painted imagery, this toy is pure magic. And for the child who is forever dreaming of flying off into the great blue yonder, this pull-along toy is a real joy.

Design and Technique Considerations

Take a look at the working drawings (Illus. 2 and 3) and see how the toy is turned, carved, whittled, and fretted. The body of the plane, the wheels, and the pop-in pilot are turned; the propeller is whittled; and all the other little bits and pieces are cut with a scroll saw.

Note how, at a scale of about two grid squares to 1″, the plane is about 12″ long from nose to tail, and 12″ wide across the wings. See, also, how the two-bladed propeller and the wheels are free-turning, and how the pilot is a loose fit in his cockpit seat.

As to the skill and technique level of the project, the only parts that could be consid-ered slightly tricky have to do with the final assembling and painting: fitting the tail in the slot, carving the propeller, and painting the imagery. All the other working stages, how-ever, are fairly straightforward.

Illus. 1. Project picture.

Tools and Materials

- An 18″ length of 3 × 3″-square beech—for the fuselage and pilot (this allows for a small amount of wastage).
- A 5″ length of 4 × 4″-square beech—for the two ground wheels (this allows for generous wastage).
- A 10″ length of 1½ × 2″, straight-grained, knot-free white pine—for the propeller.
- A sheet of best-quality ⅜″-thick, birch-faced multicore plywood—for the wings and details.
- A small scrap of best-quality plywood at ¼″ thick—for the back wheels and washers.
- A 6″ length of ⅜″-diameter dowel—for the front axle; an 18″ length of ¼″-diameter dowel—for the various struts and the back shafts; a scrap of split-down dowel—for the assembly pegs.
- The use of a lathe.
- A four-jaw chuck to fit the lathe.
- A tailstock drill chuck that is large enough to take a ⅜″-diameter drill bit.
- A good selection of turning gouges and chisels.
- A V-block and strap clamp.
- An electric scroll saw—we use a Hegner.
- A hand drill with bits at ⅛″, ¼″, ⅜″, and ½″ diameter.
- A pack of graded sandpapers.
- A straight saw.
- A coping saw.
- A ⅜″-wide chisel.
- A quantity of PVA wood glue.
- A small tube of Super Glue.
- A small knife—for whittling the propeller.
- A small hand plane.
- Acrylic paints in red, black, white, and dark blue.
- Soft-haired paint brushes: both broad and fine-point.
- A large brass screw-eye or cup hook, with a shoulder flange.
- Two brass washers—to fit the screw-eye.
- A 36″ length of woven nylon twine—for the pull-cord.

Turning the Fuselage and Pilot

When you have a good understanding of how the project needs to be made and put together, take the 18″ length of 3 × 3″-square beech and find the end center-points by setting the ends out with crossed diagonals.

Check through your pre-switch-on safety list (page 17); then set the wood securely between the chuck and the tail center, and swiftly turn it down to a 2½″-diameter cylinder. Having noted that the body of the plane and the pilot are turned all of a piece, use the rule and the callipers to set out the various step-offs that make up the design. Working from left to right, allow 1½″ for headstock chuck waste, 12″ for the fuselage, 3″ for the pilot, and a last 1½″ for tailstock waste (Illus. 4, top). Double-check to be sure that your step-offs are correct, and then register the length and diameter of the required turnings by sinking a number of pilot cuts. Working from left to right along the work-piece, sink pilot cuts on the waste side of the 1½″ waste-fuselage line, on the pilot side of the fuselage-pilot line, and finally on the waste side of the pilot-waste line. With the wood well set out, take the skew chisel and begin to work, cutting away the waste and shaping the body of the plane. It's best to strive for a long, round-nosed, slightly tapered cigar shape. Have the tail taper start about 6″ away from the nose. When you have a good fuselage form, use the point of the skew chisel to work the two V-cuts for the nose cowling.

When you are ready to turn the pilot, start by reducing the 2½″-diameter cylinder down to 1″ (Illus. 4, middle left). When this is done, mark in the position of the neck line, and then use the skew chisel to turn off the little ball-head and the cylinder-body skittle, or pin, form (Illus. 4, bottom).

Finally, sand the 1″-diameter pilot down slightly so that he is a snug fit in the 1″-diameter cockpit hole, use the very finest sandpaper to burnish the wood to a good smooth finish, and then part off the two turnings.

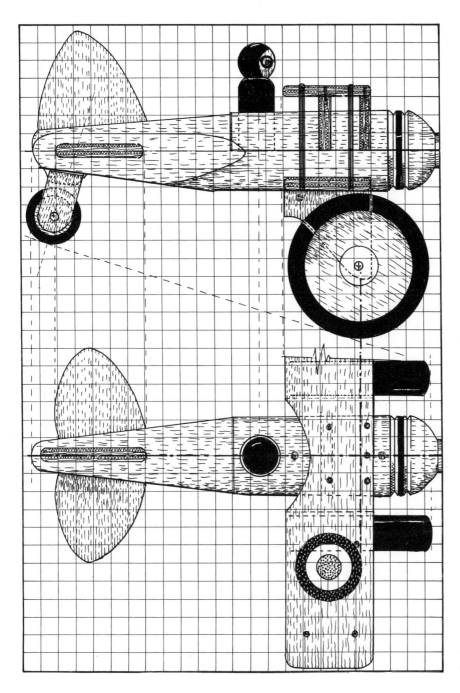

Illus. 2. Working drawings. The scale is two grid squares to 1″.

Turning the Two Large Ground Wheels

Having noted that the two large ground wheels are 4″ in diameter, 1″ thick, and round-edged, with a tire set about ½″ from the rim, and a raised central boss (Illus. 3, bottom), take the

5″ length of 4 × 4″ wood and establish the end-center points by marking the ends off with crossed diagonals. Set the wood in the chuck, bring both the tail center and the tool rest up to the wood, and switch on.

Start by swiftly turning the wood down to a smooth 4″-diameter cylinder. When this is done, take the pencil, ruler, and dividers, and

109

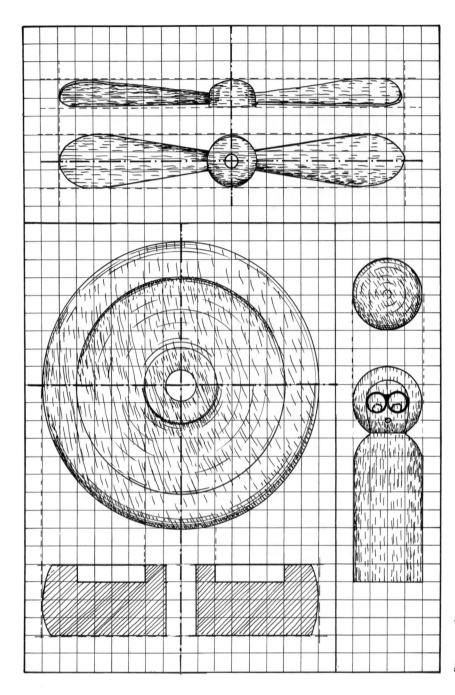

Illus. 3. Working drawings. Top: The scale is two grid squares to 1″. Bottom: The scale is four grid squares to 1″.

set the wood out with five 1″-wide step-offs: 1″ for headstock waste, 1″ for the first wheel, 1″ for between-wheel waste, 1″ for the second wheel, and a final 1″ for tailstock waste. Take the parting tool and sink pilot cuts on either side of the wheels, running the cuts about 1½″ down into the wood (Illus. 5, top left). Still working at either side of the wheels, clear away as much waste as possible until you get all the way down to the remaining 1″ core. Now take the skew chisel and, working from center to side, turn off the sharp wheel edges so as to create the beautiful, slightly curved rim profile (Illus. 5, top right).

Having achieved the basic wheel shapes, slide the tailstock center back out of the way,

110

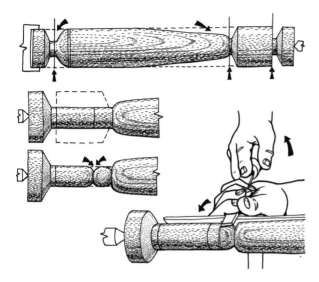

Illus. 4. Top: Set out the step-offs that go into making up the design, allowing 1½" for waste, 12" for the fuselage, 3" for the pilot, and a final 1½" for waste at the tailstock. Middle left: Turn the cylinder down to 1" for the pilot. Bottom: Use the skew chisel to turn off the little ball-head and the rounded shoulders. Place the tool on the high point of the ball, and cut with a sliding, smooth-rolling, down-in-and-up movement.

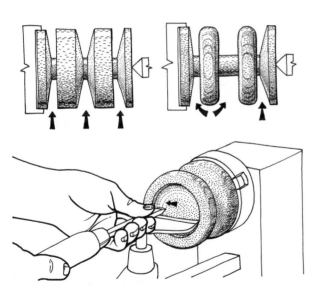

Illus. 5. Top left: Set the wood out with five 1"-wide step-offs, and use the parting tool to sink pilot cuts on either side of the wheels. Top right: Use the skew chisel to turn off the sharp edges and to create the curved profile. Remove the tailstock waste. Bottom: Lower the inside-tire face by ¼".

and reposition the tool rest over the bed of the lathe so that you can approach the wheel flat-face on. Now, having marked the ½"-wide outside rim or tire and the 1"-diameter central boss, take the tool(s) of your choice—I used a skew chisel and a parting tool—and very carefully lower the face of the wheel. Lower the inside tire face by about ¼" or until the rim and the boss are left standing in high relief (Illus. 5, bottom). Move the tool rest out of the way, fit the drill chuck and the ⅜" bit in the tailstock, and bore out the axle hole. When this is done, give the wheel a good rubbing down with the finest sandpaper and then part it off from the lathe. Repeat the procedure for the second wheel.

Shaping the Fuselage

Having first carefully studied the working drawings (Illus. 2 and 3), look at the turned fuselage nose on, and quarter-mark the cigar shape around its circumference at 12, 3, 6, and 9 o'clock, so as to establish the position of the "top," "undercarriage," and "side(s)." With the turning secured "top" side down in the V-block, take the small plane and cut away the waste between the belly and the tail (Illus. 6, top). Repeat the procedure to shape the "side" tail areas. Aim to leave the last 4 to 5" of the tail—underside and sides—looking smooth and flat-faced.

Now, having studied the working drawings and seen how the ⅜"-thick plywood tail piece is a tight push friction-fit in a body slot, use the straight saw and coping saw to work a ⅜"-wide slot that runs from top to bottom through the tail. When this is done, take the ⅜"-wide chisel and work the two ⅜"-wide blind-mortise tail-wing slots, one on each side of the tail. Have the mortises running down into the wood to a depth of about ¼".

Take the straight saw and at a position about 6½" along from the nose of the plane, run a cut halfway down through the fuselage. Be sure not to run the cut past the halfway mark.

Now muffle the turning with a binding of old rags, set it nose up in the vise, and run a saw cut down through the length of the wood to meet the halfway cut. If all is well, you should be able to remove the top front-quarter, or top-front cowling, section. With the cowling section secured flat-face down on the bench, mark in the position of the pilot's cockpit, and then use the drill and a 1″-diameter spade or sawtooth bit to run a hole through the wood. Use the graded sandpapers to leave the cockpit hole and rim looking nicely contoured and slightly funnel-shaped. When this is done, chamfer off the mating cut edges of the cowling and the undercarriage, and fit them back together with glue and wooden pegs (Illus. 6, bottom).

Finally, mark in on the undercarriage the position of the front underwing, and use the straight saw and chisel to sink the ³⁄₈″-deep, 2½″-wide wing-housing slot.

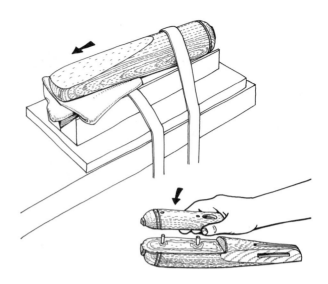

Illus. 6. Top: Secure the fuselage top-side down in the V-block strap clamp, and use a small plane to cut away the waste from between the belly and the tail. Bottom: Use glue and wooden pegs to refit the cowling section; then strap it up with masking tape and put it to one side to dry.

Fretting and Fitting the Wings, Tail, and Undercarriage

When you have studied the diagrammatic cutting grid (Illus. 7) and noted how many forms need to be cut from the ³⁄₈″-thick plywood—the two main wings, the two tail wings, the rudder-tail-wheel piece, the two distance pieces that go between the body and the top wings, and the undercarriage—trace off the profiles and pencil-press-transfer the traced shapes through to the working face of the plywood. When this is done, drill out the various holes and then use the scroll saw to cut out the profiles. Having seen how some edges need to be left square while others need to be rounded, use the rasp and the graded sandpapers to take all the cutouts to an appropriate good finish.

Take the two fretted and finished main wings, strap them together with tabs of masking tape, and use the drill and the ¼″-diameter bit to sink the six through-wing strut holes.

Having studied the working drawings and

noted how the tail pieces are fit into slots, the wings fit into either side of the fuselage, and the undercarriage built on the underside of the lower wing, drill out the various ⅛″-diameter glue-peg holes, cut little tight-fitting dowel pegs from scraps of dowel, and glue the cutouts together so as to make the basic biplane form (Illus. 8). Finally, cut the washers and the back wheel from the ¼″-thick plywood and sand the edges to a smooth round-edged finish.

Carving the Propeller

Study the various propeller drawings, if necessary make a Plasticine prototype, and consider how the propeller needs to be cut, carved, and fitted. When you have a clear understanding of how the form needs to be worked, carefully trace off the bow-tie profile. Take the piece of 1½″-wide, ¾″-thick, straight-grained, knot-free pine, locate the center-point by drawing crossed diagonals, align the tracing with the various center-lines, and pencil-press-transfer the image through to the wide flat face of the wood. Make sure that the lines are clearly established (Illus. 9, top left). Run a ¼″-diameter hole through the propeller boss for the pivot screw, and then use the scroll saw to cut out the basic propeller form.

Set the cutout down flat on the work surface so that the 10″-long shape is best-face up and aligned with the vertical axis, and then carefully shade in the top-right and bottom-left quarters. When you have shaded in one side of the cutout, flip the shape over and repeat the procedure on the other side (Illus. 9, top center). When this is done, hold the cutout secure, and use the tool of your choice—a plane, rasp, or knife—to waste and angle the

Illus. 7. Diagrammatic cutting grid. The scale is two grid squares to 1″.

shaded areas. And so you continue, turning, angling, and shaping, no matter how the wood is being held, only removing the wood waste from the top-right quarter. As you are working, try to cut diagonally across the run of the grain.

Finally, when you have achieved a good, round-ended, thin-edged form, take the graded sandpapers and rub the propeller down to a smooth finish.

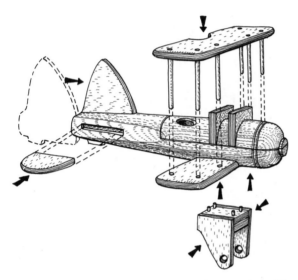

Illus. 8. Assembly. The tail pieces fit into slots. The top wing is supported on brackets, glued onto the cowling, and secured with dowel-pegs. The bottom wing is set in a slot and linked to the top wing with six dowel struts. The lower wing is glued and pegged to the undercarriage.

Putting the Piece Together

When you have made the propeller and glued and pegged the wings to the fuselage, the tail and rudder in their slots, and the undercarriage to the underside of the lower wing, turn back to the project picture (Illus. 1) and see how, by means of a large brass screw-eye or cup hook, the propeller is pivoted and the pull-cord is attached. With brass washers on either side of the propeller, run the thread of

the screw-eye or cup hook through the propeller and on through and into the nose of the fuselage. If all is well, the propeller should be an easy fit. Slide a prepared 3/8"-diameter dowel through the undercarriage axle holes, slide the washers in place, and glue the wheels on the ends of the axle. The wheels should be tightly glued on the ends of the axle, whereas the axle needs to be a loose fit in the undercarriage axle holes and the washers.

When you are about to attach the rear wheel, first use the Super Glue to fasten one of the rear wheel plates to one side of the rudder spur, then slide the wheel and the axle in position, and finally glue the other axle plate in place on the other side of the rudder spur (Illus. 9, bottom). The axle needs to be a loose fit through the wheel and a tight glued fit in the axle plates. It's best to have the axle running out about 1/2" on either side of the wheel (Illus. 9, bottom).

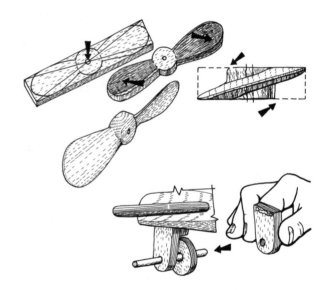

Illus. 9. Top left: Establish the center-point with crossed diagonals and press-transfer the propeller shape through to the wood. Top center: Shade in the areas that need to be cut away. Top right: A cross section showing the areas to be wasted. Bottom: Glue one wheel plate to the underside of the rudder plate, glue the length of dowel in position, slide the wheel on the dowel, and glue the other wheel plate in position.

Painting and Finishing

Now clear away all the dust, debris, and clutter, and set out your brushes, paint cans, and paints. Study Illus. 2 once more, and then, being careful not to paint the axles, holes, or washers, start by giving the whole body of the plane a thin wash of red. Apply several thin watery coats, giving the workpiece a light sanding between coats, until you have a nice, even, transparent, grain-enhancing color. When the base coat is dry, paint in all the details that make up the design: the red-white-and-blue ring markings; the black wheel tires, wing struts, pilot's helmet, goggles, and coat; the white and red centers of the wheels; and so on. When you come to painting the details, use a thick consistency of paint and a fine-point brush. Never overload the brush. When the paint is completely dry, use the finest sandpaper to rub the workpiece down to a smooth finish. Then dust the workpiece off and lay on three or more coats of clear varnish, rubbing down between coats.

Finally, knot the pull-cord onto the brass screw-eye in the middle of the propeller, and the airplane is ready for takeoff.

Hints and Modifications

- If you are at all concerned about shape and fit, it's best to make a prototype with rough wood before you begin the project.
- If you like the overall idea of the project but are not so happy about the wood turning, you could modify the details and work the airplane from a prepared length of wood, say, a piece of banister rail. You could cut the large wheels from plywood and whittle the pilot from a short length of broomstick dowel.

11
A PULL-ALONG WHITE ELEPHANT

An elephant with lever-operated up-and-down head movement

Primary techniques: flat-wood scroll-saw work, drilling, and painting

When I was a little kid, I had a real problem with pronouncing the word "elephant." I could manage "effer . . . lump" and "eller . . . fump" and all manner of stumbling lump-and-fump combinations, but somehow, I just couldn't get my lips, tongue, and brain around the word "elephant." Consequently, as much as I loved the true king of the jungle, I tended to avoid all reference to the unpronounceable beast. And then came the great day, when right out of the blue, the word trickled off my tongue like magic.

From that wonderful moment on, I became the most eloquent and enthusiastic of elephant fanciers. I would walk around the house loudly repeating the word over and over. And I read stories about elephants, drew pictures of elephants, and of course had elephant toys. My favorite elephant toy was a beautifully painted and patterned Indian type of pull-along white elephant, with lever-operated head-and-trunk movement. When the tail was pressed down, the head and trunk would lift up, and when the tail was released, the head and trunk would spring back into position. That toy was the inspiration for this project.

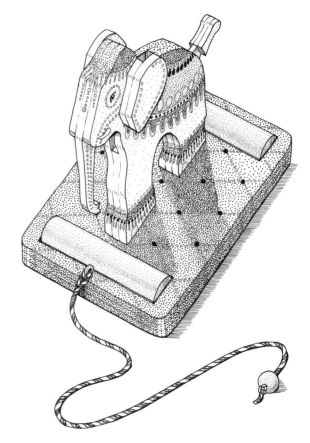

Illus. 1. Project picture.

116

Design and Technique Considerations

Take a look at the working drawings (Illus. 2) and the diagrammatic cutting grids (Illus. 3 and 4), and see how, at a scale of two grid squares to ¾", the toy is about 6" high, 9" long, and 6" wide. Study the cross-section details, and note the way the head-to-tail mechanism is pivoted and spring-loaded so that when the tail lever is released, the spring pulls the head down again.

The body is built up from three layers of ¼"-thick plywood, with the body cavity being formed by having the central sandwiched layer partially pierced and cut away. The head is built from seven layers of plywood: a central trunk, a cheek on each side of the trunk, a spacer on each side of the cheek, and an ear on each side of the spacer. The wheels are slightly unusual, in that not only are they in the form of rollers, but the rollers further connote the image of a Burmese or Indian elephant moving logs. Note the way the roller-wheels are contained in the base. All in all, it's a toy in the naïve, easy-to-make scroll-saw tradition—and the perfect starter project for beginners.

Tools and Materials

- A sheet of ¼"-thick, best-quality, white-faced multicore plywood at 18 × 18"—this allows for a generous amount of waste.
- A 7" length of 1"-diameter broomstick dowel.
- An 8" length of ¼"-diameter dowel—for the wheel and mechanism pivots and for the screw-eye driver.
- A large straight saw.
- A hammer and a handful of brass brads.
- A pair of long-nosed grips or pliers to remove the brads.
- The use of a scroll saw—we use a Hegner.
- A pencil, ruler, and compass.
- A small hand drill with bits at ⅛" and ¼".

- Super Glue.
- Three brass screw-eyes: one large and two small.
- A 1"-long low-power "pull" spring.
- A small amount of two-tube filler for nail holes.
- A pack of graded sandpapers.
- A good selection of matt acrylic paints in bright colors, including red, yellow, black, blue, green, orange, gold, and white.
- A can of clear gloss varnish.
- A couple of brushes: a broad and a fine-point.
- A length of colored cord and a ½"-diameter yellow wooden bead.

Setting Out the Design and Cutting the Base

When you have fully considered all the aspects of the project, set out your tools so that they are conveniently close at hand and check over your wood to make sure that it is free from flaws. Draw the design up to size and trace off all the profiles that go into making up the design. Spend time making sure that critical details—the pivot holes, the two elephant-to-base mortises, the curved profiles that are intended to slide against each other, and the roller-wheel slots and holes—are to size and precisely aligned.

Note: Don't draw the base details for all three layers—just for the top sheet.

Take the straight saw and, working well to the waste side of the drawn line, swiftly rough out the three pieces of plywood that make up the base sandwich. With the top sheet uppermost, sandwich the three sheets together and secure them with a couple of brads. Make sure that the brads are placed so that they are well clear of areas that are to be sawn, and with the heads sticking up so that they can easily be moved at a later stage. Having clearly established in your own mind the areas that are to be cut away, take the hand drill and the ⅛"-diameter bit and run pilot holes through the enclosed "windows," the two roller-wheel slots (Illus. 5, top left). To avoid mistakes, it's a good idea to shade in the waste areas.

When you are happy that all the base details are clearly and accurately established, move the workpiece to the scroll saw and set to work, clearing away the waste. With the sawn line always running just a little to the waste side of the drawn line, first cut out the basic round-cornered 6 × 9″ slab and then clear the waste from the enclosed roller-wheel holes. One hole at a time, release the saw-arm tension, unhitch the blade, pass the blade through the pilot hole, retension the saw arm, and then cut out the "window" (Illus. 5, top right). It's all easy enough, as long as you control the pace so that the saw blade is always clearly and timely presented with the line of the next cut. When you have finished cutting the triple-board sandwich, rub all the cut edges down to a smooth finish, remove the nails/brads, carefully ease the boards apart, and, with a pencil, label the boards "top," "middle," and "bottom."

When you have achieved three identical base boards, take the "middle" one and adjust the ends of the roller-wheel window holes by cutting the little squares that make up the dowel-pin pockets. Reckon on having the pockets centrally placed, ¼″ wide, and ¼″ deep. Then, take the "top" board and cut the two "feet" mortises (Illus. 5, bottom).

Cutting Out and Fitting the Elephant

Take another look at the working drawings (Illus. 2) and the diagrammatic cutting grids (Illus. 3 and 4), and see how the actual elephant is made up from 13 separate cutouts: two identical body sides, a single trunk-head-tail, a central two-leg spacer, a single body spacer that is set between the back of the head and the tail, two identical head-cheeks, two identical ears, two identical spacers that go

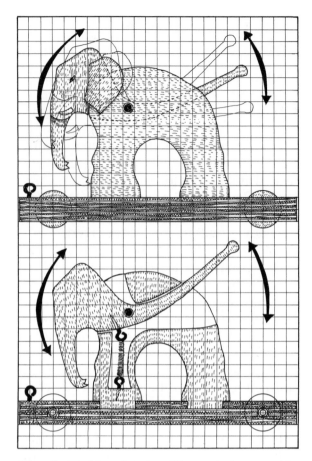

Illus. 2. Working drawing. The scale is two grid squares to ¾″.

between the cheeks and the ears, and two identical side-of-tail pieces. Pencil-press-transfer the 13 profiles through to the working face of the plywood, and use the scroll saw to swiftly cut the wood down to the 13 component parts. Again, make sure that you stay well to the waste side of the drawn lines.

Pair up the matching parts—the two ears, the two side-bodies, and so on—and attach each pair with a couple of brads or nails (Illus. 6, top). As with the base pieces, make sure that the brads or nails are well away from the areas to be worked—the cutting lines and the pivot holes—and that the heads are sticking up. When this is done, go back to the scroll saw and carefully cut out both the single-layer and the double-layer profiles. When you have

Illus. 3. Diagrammatic cutting grid. The scale is two grid squares to ¾".

achieved the cutouts, remove the brads or nails (Illus. 6, bottom) and, with a pencil, label all the parts, such as "right-ear outside face," "left-ear outside face," and so on. If necessary, sand the rough edges smooth.

Having studied the working-drawing details at the bottom of Illus. 2 and seen how the body of the elephant is made up from two central pieces that are sandwiched between the sides, trace off the position of the two spacer pieces and pencil-press-transfer the traced lines through to the inside face of one or other of the side-body pieces. Now, with the body piece set down on the work surface so that the inside-face is uppermost, carefully place and align the spacers with the pencilled guidelines. If necessary, check the fit by making sure that the trunk-head-tail piece is able to move through its arc. When you are pleased that all is correct, fit the screw-eye in position at the bottom of the front-leg cavity. First make a starter hole, with a long nail or spike. Now, having cut a groove in the end of a length of dowel, fit the screw-eye in the slot (Illus. 7, top left) and use the dowel to drive the screw-eye into position (Illus. 7, top right). Use the Super Glue to stick the spacer pieces permanently in position.

Take a look at the elephant's head-tail piece, and see the way the head is built from seven layers: the central trunk-head-tail, the cheeks on either side of the head, and the spacers

Illus. 4. Diagrammatic cutting grid. The scale is two grid squares to ¾".

120

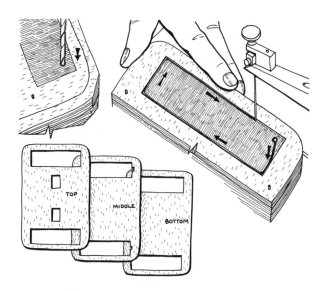

Illus. 5. Top left: Shade in the areas of waste. Then
drill a pilot hole into the waste and through the
three layers of plywood. Top right: Pass the saw
blade through the pilot hole, retension the blade,
and cut on the waste side of the drawn line.
Bottom: The three base boards: the "top" with the
two foot mortise holes, the "middle" with the
roller-wheel dowel-pin pockets, and the "bottom"
with the roller-wheel holes.

and ears on either side of the cheeks. Note,
also, how the tail handle is built up from three
layers: the central tail that runs through from
the head, and the two small side pieces. Take
the various cutouts and have a trial dry-run
fitting. Make sure that the edge profiles all
come together for a good fit, paying particular
attention to the ear spacers and where the
curve of the body fits and slides against the
curve of the cheeks. Once you have fitted,
adjusted, sanded, and refitted, take the Super
Glue and carefully sandwich up the layers.
Don't forget the two small side-of-tail pieces.
Wait a short while for the glue to set, and then
use the sandpaper to reduce the thickness of
the in-body areas of the head-tail piece, meaning the sliding, or moving, parts that are contained in the body cavity. Aim to reduce the
$\frac{1}{4}$″ thickness by about $\frac{1}{16}$″ (Illus. 7, bottom).

When you have built the seven-layer head,
mark in on the head-tail piece and on the side

panels the position of the dowel-pivot hole.
Double-check to be sure that the hole centers
are perfectly placed; then take the hand drill
and the $\frac{1}{4}$″-diameter bit and bore out the
holes. If you are at all worried about alignment, it would be a good idea to drill the head-
tail piece out first and then to use the hole to
confirm the placing of the side-panel holes
(Illus. 8, top).

Use a scrap of sandpaper to make the head-
tail hole a loose fit on a $\frac{1}{4}$″-diameter dowel.
When you have bored out the three pivot
holes, check the position by sandwiching the
toy together and running the dowel through
the pivot hole. If all is well, when the tail is
pressed down, the movement should be
smooth, easy, and friction-free.

Fit the screw-eye into the thickness of the
head-tail piece, and hook the spring between
the two screw-eyes. Make sure that the spring
is secure.

Finally, fit the trunk-head-tail piece inside
the body cavity, slide the dowel-pivot through

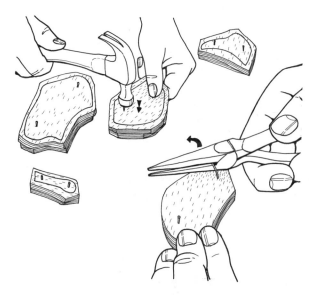

Illus. 6. Top: Pair up the matching components and
attach them together with brads or nails, making
sure that they are well away from the cutting lines
and are left with their heads protruding. Bottom:
When the parts have been cut, use the grips to
remove the brads or nails, rolling the grips over so
as not to damage the wood.

the three layers, have a last check to make sure that the seesaw movement of the head and tail is still easy, and then glue the body sides and the dowel ends.

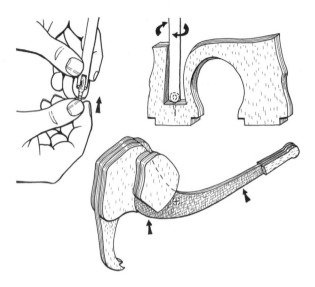

Illus. 7. Top left: To make a screw-eye driver, cut a slot in the end of a length of dowel. The screw-eye needs to be a wedge-fit. Top right: Position the screw-eye in the base of the front-leg cavity and drive it into place with the dowel-tool. Bottom: Sand the shaded areas, reducing the thickness by about 1/16".

Fitting the Roller-Wheels and the Elephant

Study Illus. 2 once more, and see how the roller-wheels are made up from lengths of 1"-diameter broomstick dowel set and pivoted within 1¼"-wide base slots. Note the way the pivots are made from short lengths of ¼"-diameter dowel that are tapped into the ends of the rollers and loosely contained by the three sandwiched sheets that make up the base.

Cut the 1"-diameter dowel into two 2⅞" lengths, and rub the cut ends and edges down with the sandpaper until they are smooth. Establish the position of the end-centers, and run ¼"-diameter holes into the dowel ends to a depth of about ½".

Do this with all four dowel-ends. Cut four ¾" lengths of ¼"-diameter dowel, rub the dowel-ends down slightly, cut a small glue-groove along the in-roller end, smear glue over the grooved end, and push them home into the roller holes (Illus. 8, bottom). Note: If you want the rollers painted, rather than left plain, this is the time to do it.

With the three base sheets labelled "top," "middle," and "bottom," take the middle and bottom sheets and carefully glue them together. Now, having rubbed the protruding end-of-roller dowel-pins down so that they are slightly less than ¼" in diameter, set them in the roller-wheel holes so that the dowel-ends are contained in the little pockets. Having made sure that the two foot mortises are a good fit, take the "top" layer of the base, smear glue over the mating faces, and set it in position so as to complete the three-layer sandwich. Rub the foot tenons down until they are a tight push-fit in the base mortises and glue the elephant in position.

Once the glue is set, fill the holes left by the pins and rub the whole toy down to a good finish in readiness for painting.

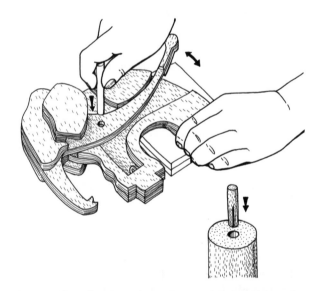

Illus. 8. Top: Support the side panel on a piece of scrap plywood, place the head piece in position, and use a scrap of dowel to confirm the placing of the holes. Bottom right: Smear glue on the dowel-ends and tap them into the end-of-roller holes.

Painting and Finishing

When you have a well-fitting, easy-moving toy, then comes the enjoyable task of painting and decorating. Take a look at the project picture (Illus. 1) and the painting grid (Illus. 9), and see how the elephant has been given a royal Indian type of imagery, with lots of brightly painted patterns and tassels. The elephant is white, the base is red, and the details are brought out in such colors as red, yellow, orange, green, and metallic gold. It's best to start off by applying the large areas of color, and then to paint the small details. When the paint is dry, lay on a couple of coats of varnish. Be careful not to gum up the works by getting blobs of paint or varnish on the moving parts.

Finally, fit the large screw-eye on the base at the front, tie on the colored pull-cord and the yellow bead, and the wonderful Indian effer . . . eller . . . lump is complete.

Hints and Modifications

- If you like the idea of the toy but want to change the scale and make an elephant that is, say, twice the size, use ½″-thick plywood, larger-diameter roller-wheel pins, and a stronger spring.
- If you don't have the use of a scroll saw, you can use either a coping saw or a fretsaw. You would have to cut the pieces out individ-

Illus. 9. Painting grid. The scale is two grid squares to ¾″.

ually and rub them down to a good fit and match.
- If you don't like the idea of using springs, you could leave them out and create a more basic push-down pull-up movement.

12
A PULL-ALONG SET OF SOLDIER SKITTLES

A set of soldier skittles, or pins, loosely mounted on a wheeled base

Primary techniques: turning, boring holes, shaping, and painting

Children have always enjoyed playing knock-over skittles, otherwise known, from country to country, as skittle-ball, pinball, ninepins, tenpins, quilles, kegelspiel, kayles, and lawn bowling. The skittles, or pins, are set up in formation and then knocked down with a ball. The players try to knock down as many pins as possible with as few balls as possible. Certainly, the rules as to lineups and distances vary depending upon where you are playing, but the basic game is the same.

The inspiration for our skittles is drawn directly from what our late Victorian great great grandparents would have called "drawing room," "captain," or "soldier" skittles. Turned all of a piece and decorated with soldier imagery of the period, such skittles were made first in Germany and then later in America by German toymakers in Pennsylvania.

Design and Technique Considerations

Take a look at the working drawings (Illus. 2 and 3) and see how, at a grid scale of four squares to 1″, the nine soldier pins are just a shade under 1″ in diameter and about 8″ high, while the round-ended 1½″-thick base slab is 9″ long and 5″ wide. The four shop-bought

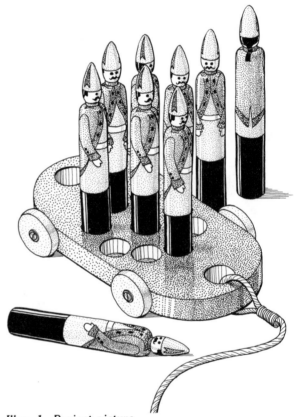

Illus. 1. Project picture.

wheels are screwed directly to the sides of the base slab, with washers between the screw head and the wheel, and between the wheel and the sides of the base.

Note the circular arrangement of the pins on the slab, with the hole-centers being set, one at the middle of, and the other eight at 45° intervals around, the circumference of a 3½"-diameter circle. All the holes are 1" in diameter, with the pin holes being ¾" deep, and the holes for the pull-cord set on the center-line and run right through the thickness of the slab. It's fair to say that the only tricky part of the project is making the repeated shapes on the lathe, which requires very careful measuring.

The inspiration for the soldiers' uniforms is drawn from the mercenary soldiers of the American Revolution, or to be more specific, from grenadier soldiers of the von Rall Hessian regiment. The design of the toy is such, that between games, the soldiers can be set and stored in formation on the wheeled base and towed around the playroom.

Tools and Materials

- A slab of 1½"-thick beech that is 10" long and 5" wide—for the base slab (this allows for a small amount of end waste).
- Twelve 10" lengths of 1 × 1"-square beech for the pins (this allows for three spares in case of mistakes and playing breakages).
- Four 2"-diameter wheels, with four 1½"- to 2"-long brass round-head screws and eight washers to fit.
- A pencil, ruler, and try square.
- A compass.
- The use of an electric scroll saw—we use a Hegner.
- A drill press with a 1"-diameter flat or spade bit.
- The use of a lathe.
- A selection of turning tools, including a skew chisel and a thinly bladed parting tool.
- A pair each of dividers and callipers.
- A pack of graded sandpapers.
- A ball of string and a pack of thumbtacks—for the drying line.

- A small can of matt white undercoat.
- Acrylic paints in black, red, blue, and yellow.
- A can of clear varnish.
- A couple of soft-haired paint brushes: a broad and a fine-point.
- A 36" length of soft ¼"-diameter rope—for the pull-cord.

Setting Out the Base Slab

When you have studied the design (Illus. 2 and 3), considered various modification options, and generally familiarized yourself with the project, take the 1½"-thick, 9 × 5" slab of beech and check it over for problems. Ideally, the wood should be completely free from knots, end splits, and warps. Be on the lookout for end splits that look as if they might well travel deeply into the wood.

When you are satisfied that your wood is sound, set it best-face up and down flat on the work surface. Use the try square and ruler to square off the end waste; then establish the 9" length of the slab and locate the center-point by drawing crossed diagonals. When this is done, draw in a center-line that divides the 5" width and runs the full length of the wood. Next, with the compass set to a radius of 1¾", spike the point on the center-point of the slab and draw out a 3½"-diameter circle. Use the compass and the try square to establish at 45° intervals around the circle the position of the eight pin holes (Illus. 4, bottom). Measure 2½" along from each end of the slab, and use the square to establish across the width of the slab the wheel stub-axle center-lines. Run the lines right around the slab, including down the thickness and across the underside (Illus. 4, top). At one end of the slab, set the compass to a radius of 2½", spike the point on the stub-axle center-line intersection, and scribe out the 5"-diameter half-circle that sets the shape of the end of the slab. Do this with both ends.

Then, by measuring 1" away from the ends

of the slab, mark the position on the center-line of the two pull-cord holes.

Scroll Sawing and Drilling

When you have established the shape of the base slab and the position of the eleven 1"-diameter holes on the slab—nine for the pins and two for the pull-cord—double-check to make sure that everything is correct. Then move the workpiece to the scroll saw and cut out the round-ended profile. Working a little to the waste side of the drawn line, hold the slab firmly down on the cutting table and slowly pivot the wood so that the saw blade is always presented with the line of the next

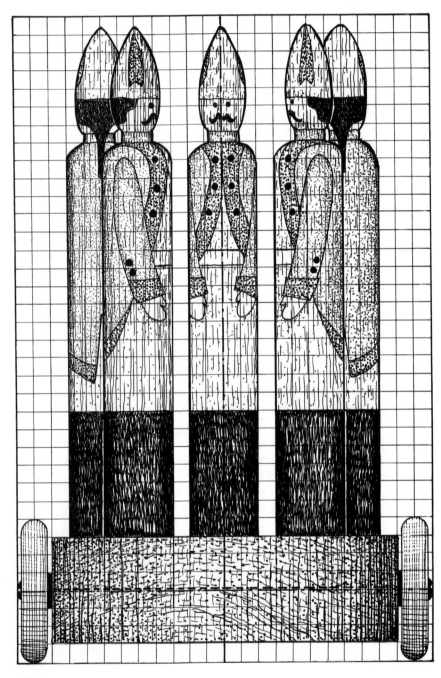

Illus. 2. Working drawing. The scale is four grid squares to 1".

cut and so that the cut is moving in a clockwise direction around the profile. If the blade is well tensioned and the wood is turned with a firmly controlled movement, the cut edge should be at a sharp 90° to the working face.

When you have achieved the boat-shaped profile, move the workpiece to the drill press. Fit the 1″-diameter bit in the drill, and, at a point ¾″ up from the horizontal cutting edge, wrap a strip of masking tape around the bit. The strip of tape acts as a depth gauge, in that it enables you to see at a glance when you have bored down to a depth of ¾″. Run through a few test borings on a scrap of wood, adjusting the depth guide until you are able to bore out holes that are perfect every time.

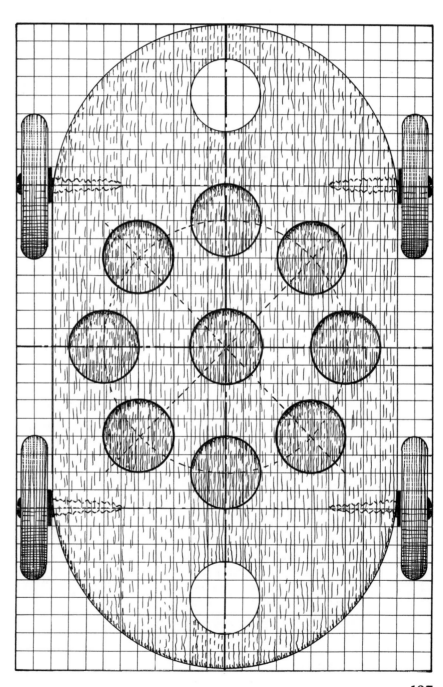

Illus. 3. Working drawing. The scale is four grid squares to 1″.

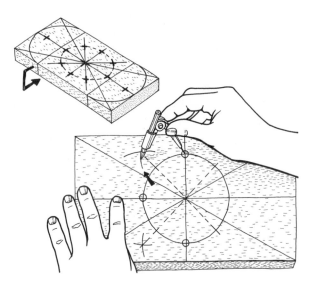

Illus. 4. Bottom: Establish the position of the nine center-points. Top: Measure and mark in the position of the axles, running the lines right around the faces and sides of the slab. Draw in the 5"-diameter half-circles at each end of the base, and mark in the position of the center-line and the pull-cord holes.

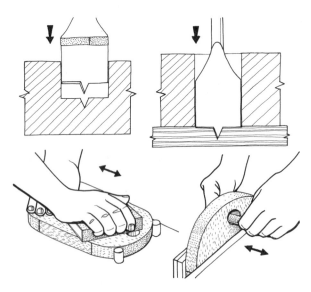

Illus. 5. Top left: Use masking tape on the drill as a depth gauge, and run the hole down to a depth of ¾". Top right: Support the workpiece on scrap wood and drill right through the 1½" thickness. Bottom left: Hold the base firmly against the bench stops, and use a sanding block to rub the surface down smooth. Bottom right: Clean the holes using a dowel and sandpaper.

Then set to work, boring out the nine pin holes. Work at an easy controlled pace, aiming for holes that are ¾" deep and crisp-edged (Illus. 5, top left). When you have worked the nine pin holes, remove the depth-gauge tape, support the workpiece on a slab of scrap wood, and run the pull-cord holes right through the 1½" thickness (Illus. 5, top right).

Then use the graded sandpapers to rub the whole workpiece down to a smooth, slightly round-edged finish (Illus. 5, bottom).

Turning the Soldier Pins

Look back at Illus. 2 and see how the 10" length of 1 × 1"-square wood allows for an inch of waste at each end of the turning. Note, also, that by turning off twelve pins—three more than you need—you will be able to select the best-matched group of nine. If you are at all concerned about being able to turn repeated shapes on the lathe, make a simple cardboard template with all the initial step-offs and measurements clearly marked.

Take a length of wood and locate the end-centers by drawing crossed diagonals. Now, having checked through your pre-switch-on safety list (page 17), set the wood securely between lathe centers, bring the tool rest up to the wood, and arrange all your tools so that they are comfortably close at hand. When you are satisfied that all is as it should be, switch on the power and use a round-nosed gouge to swiftly turn the wood down to a smooth 1" cylinder. When this is done, use the rule and dividers to mark the wood off, from left to right along its length, with the following step-offs: 1" for the headstock waste, 6¼" for the body of the soldier, ³⁄₁₆" for the neck band, 1⁹⁄₁₆" for the head, and finally 1" for the tailstock waste (Illus. 6, top). It's best to first draw out the measurements on a simple cardboard "step-off" template, and then to use this to transfer the measurements through to the wood (Illus. 6, bottom).

Working at the tailstock end of the wood, use the skew chisel to turn the waste and the

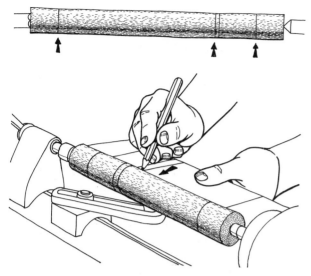

Illus. 6. Top: Mark off 1" for the headstock waste, 6¼" for the body, 3/16" for the neck, 1⁹/16" for the head, and a last 1" for the tailstock waste. Bottom: Use a simple cardboard template to transfer the design through to the wood.

head and neck down until they are reduced to a diameter of ¾" (Illus. 7). Reestablish the neck, head, and waste step-offs, and then use the tip of the skew chisel and perhaps also a thinly bladed parting tool to turn the 3/16"-wide

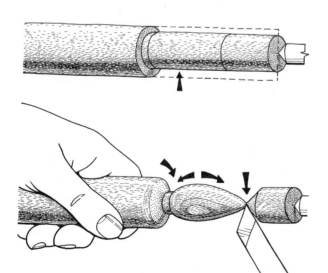

Illus. 7. Top: Turn the neck, head, and tailstock waste down to ¾". Bottom: Support the pin with your left hand, while parting off the hat with the point of the skew chisel.

band or step-off that makes up the neck of the soldier down to a diameter of about ⅝". When this is done, use the skew chisel to part off the curves at both the shoulders and the top of the neck. Aim, by working with the grain from peaks in towards valleys, to run both the 1" diameter of the body and the ¾" diameter of the head in a smooth curve into each side of the 3/16"-wide neck band.

Once the shoulders and face are smoothly curved, turn your attention to the soldier's hat. At a point about an inch down from the tip, use the skew chisel to cut away the waste and to turn down the smoothly curved, characteristically pointed-arch shape of the hat, leaving a small stem of waste to be turned off later. Use the skew chisel to slightly reduce the diameter of the bottom of the soldier. Aim for a diameter that is slightly smaller than an inch—say, about ⅞".

Rub the whole workpiece down with the graded sandpapers, and use the point of the skew chisel to part off from the lathe. Cut most of the way through between the bottom of the pin and the headstock; then support and cup the pin with your left hand, while at the same time using the point of the skew chisel to carefully shape and part off the hat. Finally, complete the parting off at the foot and rub the base down with the sandpaper (Illus. 7, bottom). Repeat this procedure with all twelve pins.

Painting and Finishing

When you have achieved the base slab and nine well-matched pins, wipe off the dust and move them to the area that you have set aside for painting. Start by setting up the knotted-string drying line, spreading newspaper over the work surface, and putting out your tools and materials. Press a thumbtack into the base of each pin to be painted, and hang them upside down from the line (Illus. 8, left). Being careful not to leave blobs and runs, dip each pin head-first into the white matt undercoat, so as to leave 2½" at the foot of the pin unpainted. When the white paint is dry, first check for any buildup or dribbles and, if necessary, carefully sand back; then dip the point of each soldier's head (the cap) into the yellow paint to a depth of 1″. When the yellow paint is dry, untie the string and remove the thumbtack, and hang each pin, by a noose around its neck, the right way up on the line. Next, dip the foot of each pin into the black paint to a depth of 2¾″ (Illus. 8, middle). The black should overlap the white by a uniform margin of ¼″. It's important that, between painting stages, you check for dribbles, runs, and buildup, and, if necessary, rub back to a smooth finish.

When you have established the main areas of ground color—the black boots, white body, and yellow hat—take a soft pencil and draw in all the other features that make up the design. It's best to work from soldier to soldier, drawing in all the whiskers, all the belts, all the

arms, and so on. Working in this manner, you will be able to achieve, by way of repetition, a high degree of uniformity.

Once you have drawn in the details, use a fine-point brush to block in the colors. Start with the relatively large areas of color: the blue coats and the yellow trousers. Then, when the paint is dry, finish up with the smaller details on the faces and uniforms: black for the buttons, eyes, moustache, and hair, and the red details on the hat, collar, and cuffs (Illus. 8, right). Being careful not to dribble paint in the pin holes, paint the top and sides of the base red. When the paint is dry, give the entire workpiece—all the soldiers and the base—a thin coat of clear varnish.

Note: Be warned—if you apply the paint or varnish in thick daubs, or paint inside the pin holes, there is a risk that the soldiers will be a tight fit and impossible to remove.

Finally, using the axle center-lines on the underside of the base as a guide, screw the wheels in place on the sides of the base slab, knot the pull-cord through one of the holes, set the pins in place on the slab, and the soldiers are ready for action.

Hints and Modifications

- If you like the idea of pins but are not so keen on turning, then you could buy a length of turned broomstick dowel and just whittle the heads.
- If you would rather not use soldiers, you could have a family—granny, grandpa, mom, dad, and three kids—or perhaps you could make historical characters.
- If you like turning, then you could take the project further and turn wheels and a ball.
- You could modify the design, by painting the pins solid colors and numbering them.
- If you don't have a scroll saw, the base can be worked with a bow saw or even a straight saw and Surform rasp.

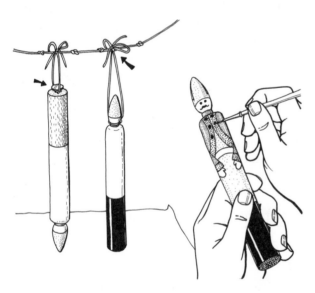

Illus. 8. Left: Press a thumbtack into the base of each pin, and then hang them from a drying line, making sure they don't touch. Middle: Remove the thumbtacks and hang the pins on the line with a noose around their neck. Right: Paint the small details: the eyes, moustache, hair, and buttons.

13

A PULL-ALONG "OLD WOMAN WHO LIVED IN A SHOE"

A toy with crank-operated side-to-side movement

Primary techniques: turning between centers, flat-wood fretwork, whittling, gluing and pegging, attaching a Z-crank, and painting

Humpty Dumpty sat on the wall . . . Hickory dickory dock . . . Baa, baa, black sheep. . . . Children love nursery rhymes—the constant repetition, the odd words, the strange notions,

Illus. 1. Project picture.

and the colorful phrases. They conjure up all kinds of wonderful mind pictures.

Most nursery rhymes are curious and appealing, but one of the strangest must surely be: "There was an old woman who lived in a shoe. . . ." When I was a child, I had a picture book with this nursery rhyme that showed a large-bosomed woman, complete with a mop bonnet, a boot-shaped house, and lots of children. It used to puzzle me as to why anyone would be living in a boot. Did it keep the rain out? Was it comfortable? Were there stairs? Why was she living in a boot rather than, say, a barrel or a box?

Take a look at the project picture (Illus. 1). Although undoubtedly strange, this toy is a real beauty. As the boot is pulled along, the old woman slowly turns from side to side. And the little peg children can be changed around in their little holes.

Design and Technique Considerations

Take a good look at the working drawings, the details, and the step-by-step instructional illustrations, and see how the toy is made and put together. See how, at a scale of one grid square to 1″ (Illus. 2) and two grid squares to 1″ (Illus. 3), the toy is about 12″ high, 12″ long, and 8″ wide. Note the way the body of the boot is made up of two turnings that have been cut, trimmed, jointed, and mounted on a plywood "sole." Look closely at the details on the bottom right of Illus. 2, and study the way the Z-crank is located in the slotted end of the bottom of the shaft that goes through the boot, to give the woman her side-to-side movement. The drive mechanism is delightfully simple and direct. As the toy is pulled along, the wheels turn the back axle, which sets the Z-crank in motion, which joggles the vertical shaft through the boot, which in turn sets the old woman's head, shoulders, and bead-weighted arms swinging from side to side.

The toy is made up from 22 turnings: the barbell shape for the front and back of the boot, a truncated cone for the upper boot, four discs with decorative recesses for the wheels, the pin-like form for the old woman, and the 15 ball-pegs for the children. When you come to making the boot, all you do is make a V-block to hold the turning, and then slice off various pieces from the barbell shape, mount the cone on one sliced face, and peg and glue the entire form on a plywood "sole." The boot is mounted on the base, and the various holes are bored out. It's all pretty straightforward, although the drive shaft and the Z-bent crank both need to be made and fitted with care.

Once you have a clear understanding of how the project needs to be worked, sit down with a pencil and work-out paper and draw the designs up to size.

Tools and Materials

- A piece of prepared 1″-thick wood that is 13″ long and 7″ wide—for the base (this allows for some wastage).
- A sheet of best-quality, ½″-thick multicore plywood that is 20″ long and 5″ wide—for the "sole" and the base plate under the axle (you could use a thinner sheet for the base plate).

- A piece of 4 × 4″-square beech that is about 36″ long—for the various turnings (you could save costs by using smaller off-cuts for one or two of the individual turnings).
- Two red beads—for the hands.
- A length of cord—for the arms and the pull-cord.
- A pencil, ruler, and work-out paper.
- The use of a lathe.
- A good selection of turning tools.
- A pair each of compasses, callipers, and dividers.
- A small straight saw.
- A V-block, made to fit the turning.
- A knife.
- A coping or scroll saw.
- Two 10″ lengths of ³⁄₁₆″ coat-hanger wire—for the axle rods.
- A pair of pliers—for bending the rod.
- Two-tube resin glue—for attaching the wheels.
- A drill with a good selection of drill bits to fit, plus a Forstner type of drill to bore out flat-bottomed holes—for the ball-peg children.
- Arcylic paints in bright bold colors.
- All the usual workshop items, such as screwdrivers, screws, sandpaper, glue, and disposable paint cans.

Preparing the Wood for the Lathe and Roughing Out

When you have a good picture in your mind's eye of how you want the project to be, pin up all the designs and drawings on the wall and clear your workshop so that you can begin. Starting with the barbell-shaped boot piece, take a 12″ length of the 4 × 4″-square beech, and check it over to make sure that it is free from splits, dead knots, stains, and waney edges.

Find the end-centers by drawing crossed diagonals on the squarely cut ends of the wood. Set the compass to a radius of 2″, and then set the ends of the wood out with scribed circles at 4″ in diameter. Pencil in tangents at the diagonal-to-circle crossover points, and establish the areas of waste by drawing lines from the resultant octagons and down the length of the wood. Use a plane to swiftly clear away the bulk of the waste until the wood is more or less octagonal.

Having made sure that the lathe is in good safe condition, mount the wood between centers and secure the workpiece by running the tailstock into the wood. Position the tool rest so that it is as close as possible to the work and slightly below the center-line. Making sure that your hair, cuffs, and such are all out of harm's way (see the checklist on page 17),

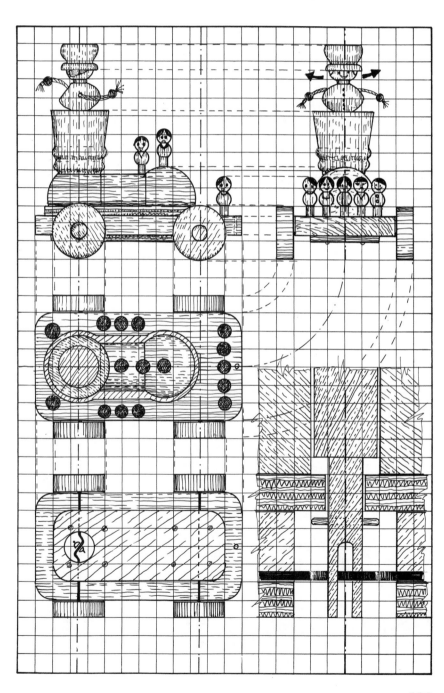

Illus. 2. Working drawings. The scale is one grid square to 1", except at the bottom right, where it is four grid squares to 1".

switch on the power. Take the large round-nosed gouge and swiftly rough the wood down to a smooth 4″-diameter cylinder.

Turning the Barbell Profile

When you have achieved the 4″-diameter cylinder, take the ruler, pencil, and dividers, and establish the center-point by making a mark 6″ away from one end of the wood. Now, starting from the center-point and working back towards the headstock, make step-offs at 1¼″, 1⅜″, and 1⅞″. If you do this on both sides of the center-point, you should be left with about 1¼″ of waste at each end of the wood. When this is done, take the parting tool and sink ⅜″-

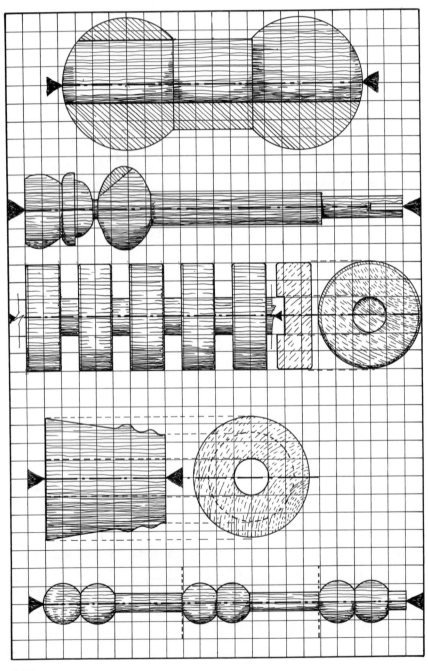

Illus. 3. Working drawings. The scale is two grid squares to 1″.

134

deep pilot depth guides into the wood at either side of the two "ball" areas (Illus. 4, top). Make sure that the cuts occur on the waste sides of the lines, that is, in the waste at the ends and in between the balls.

With the depth of waste clearly set out with the pilot cuts, take a skew chisel and set about lowering the waste between the balls. Don't be in too much of a hurry; it's best to take it little by little, all the while gradually getting closer and closer to the desired form. When you have turned it down to the 2½" diameter of the "neck" between the balls, use the various marked step-offs and pilot guides to work the part-balls that make up the ends. Although you need to aim for true spheres that are about 3¾" in diameter, don't forget that the line of the sphere will be interrupted by the 2½"-diameter cylinder that is the neck between the balls (Illus. 4, bottom left). Run the skew chisel from high to low wood, all the while aiming for a smoothly profiled sphere.

When you have turned off the barbell form, use the skew chisel to bring the wood to a

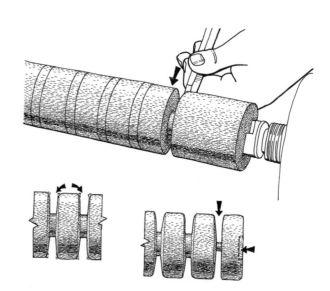

Illus. 5. Top: Use the parting tool to sink the ½"-wide waste areas to a depth of 1". Bottom left: Cut the sharp angles away with the skew chisel. Bottom right: Sink the recess in the center of the wheel to a depth of about ¼" and then part off.

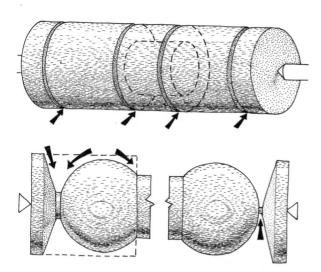

Illus. 4. Top: Use the parting tool to sink ³⁄₈"-deep pilot cuts on either side of the two "ball" areas. Bottom left: To work the two part-balls, run the skew chisel from high to low wood. Bottom right: Use the parting tool to part the work off from the lathe. Note: The waste is angled so that the tool does not bind and burn the wood.

good finish and part the workpiece off from the lathe. Along the way, you will need to widen various cuts so that the tool does not bind into the wood and burn (Illus. 4, bottom right).

Turning the Wheels

Take a 9" length of 4 × 4"-square wood and prepare it as already described, that is, mark it out, clear away the waste, mount it in the lathe, and turn it down to a smooth 3"-diameter cylinder. When this is done, take the pencil, ruler, and dividers, and starting at the headstock with a 3" length of waste, set the wood out with alternating five 1" step-offs for the wheels, and then six ½" step-offs for the between-wheel waste. Use the parting tool to sink the ½"-wide waste areas to a depth of 1" (Illus. 5, top). When you have established the width of the wheels, use the skew chisel to cut away the sharp angles. Don't round the corners over too much; just aim for a small bevel (Illus. 5, bottom left).

Once you have cut the bevels, remove the wood from between the lathe centers and remount it in a jaw chuck. Move the tailstock well out of the way, and reposition the tool rest so that you can work the wood end on. Having made sure that the lathe is correctly set up, use the skew chisel to cut away the waste. Skim the face of the first wheel down to a smooth finish. When you are satisfied with the face of the wheel, mark in a 1"-diameter circle at the center, sink the recess by about ¼", and then part off (Illus. 5, bottom right). And so you continue, facing up the next wheel, cutting the central recess, and parting off, until you have five wheels. Choose the best four.

Turning the Cone-Shaped Top of the Boot, the Woman, and the Children

Having studied the truncated cone in Illus. 3, cut a 6" length of 4 × 4"-square wood and prepare it for the lathe, as already described. Secure the wood between lathe centers and swiftly turn it down to a smooth 4"-diameter cylinder. With the measure, pencil, and dividers, mark the wood from left to right with these step-offs: 1¼" for the headstock waste, 3½" for the cone, and 1¼" for the tailstock waste.

Making sure that you keep to the waste side of the step-off marks, take the parting tool and sink a ¼"-deep depth guide at each end of the cone. The bottom-of-sinking diameter should measure 3½". Now, bearing in mind that the taper from one end of the cone down to the other needs to include the two "ripples," use a skew chisel and a small round-nosed gouge to clear away the waste. The final cone shape needs to be 3½" long and 3½" in diameter at one end and 2½" in diameter at the other. When you have what you consider is a well-turned form, part off the waste and remove the workpiece from the lathe.

When you come to working the old woman and the children, prepare, mount, mark off, and turn the wood as already described. How-ever, since these forms are smaller and more delicate, they need to be worked with extra care. You will need to support the wood as the turning progresses. And, of course, the nearer you get to completion, the more careful you need to be.

Cutting and Fitting the Boot and the Old Woman

When you have completed all the turnings that make up the design, study Illus. 6 and note the construction details. Take the barbell shape, clearly label the form "front" and "back," and then set to work with a pencil and ruler, marking the areas that need to be cut away (Illus. 3, top). You need to remove two areas: the top of the curve at the "back," and the whole underside from a point about ½" down from the center-line. Take a scrap of wood and make a V-block to support the workpiece. Have the block at about 2 × 2 × 2", with the point of the 'V' being about ½" up from the base line. Secure the block with screws (Illus. 7, top right). When you have established the areas that need to be cut away, hold the workpiece in the V-block and use a straight saw to clear away the waste (Illus. 7, top left).

Rub the sawn faces down to a smooth finish, and then take the cone that makes up the top of the boot and carefully glue and peg it in position on the main body of the boot (Illus. 7, bottom left). When the glue is dry, take the drill and a long-shafted 1"-diameter spade bit, and run a hole right down through the center of the cone and on through the boot. Spend time at this stage making sure that the hole is straight and true (Illus. 7, bottom right).

Set the boot down flat on the multicore plywood, and pencil around it so as to mark out a "sole" that is between ¼ and ½" wider all around than the boot. Fret the shape out with the coping saw, and rub the sawn edges down with the graded sandpaper. Locate the sole on the boot, and establish the position of the shaft hole. Use a ½″-diameter bit to drill out the hole. When you are happy with the fit, glue and screw the sole to the boot. Take a knife and remove the waste from the old woman's back (Illus. 6). When this is done, run a ¼″-diameter hole through the shoulders of the old woman, attach the cord-and-bead arms, and secure with glue and slivers of wood. Finally,

cut the crank-shaft location slot in the end of the woman's drive shaft (Illus. 8, left), drill out the hole, slide the shaft through the boot, and secure with a wooden peg (Illus. 8, right).

Building the Base

First cut the 1″-thick slab to size. Use the com-

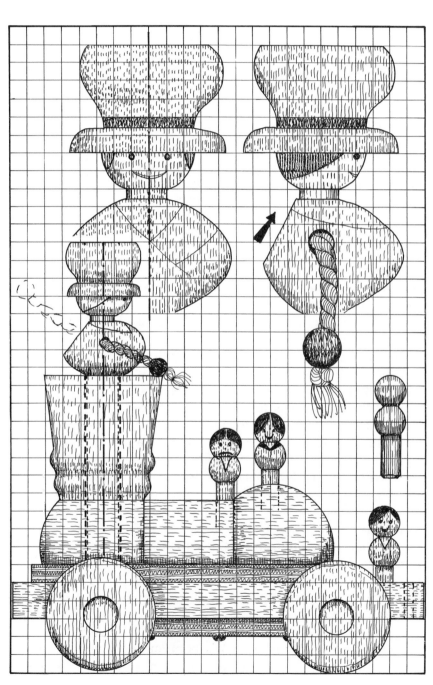

Illus. 6. Working drawing. Top: The scale is four grid squares to 1″. Bottom: The scale is two grid squares to 1″.

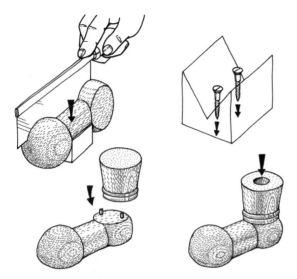

Illus. 7. Top right: Make a V-block at 2 × 2 × 2″, with the point of the "V" ½″ from the bottom; then secure it to the workbench with a couple of screws. Top left: Hold the piece in the V-block, and use the straight saw to clear away the waste. Bottom left: Glue and peg the cone to the boot. Bottom right: Use a long-shafted 1″-diameter spade or flat bit to bore a hole right down through the boot.

pass to mark in the 1″-diameter quarter-circle corners, and clear away the waste with the coping saw. Mark in the position of the boot on the base, the through-base crank hole, and the under-base axle slots (Illus. 2, bottom left). Bore the hole out with a 1¾″-diameter spade bit. Having made sure that the axle housing channels are perfectly placed in relationship to each other and to the hole, clear the channels out with a straight saw and a small chisel until they are ¼″ wide and ¼″ deep. When this is done, take the drill, a ⅛″ drill bit, and a countersink bit, and run four holes for screws through from the underside of the base slab. When you come to making the plywood plate under the axle, repeat the procedure for making the base as already described, but make the plate smaller and eliminate the axle channels (Illus. 2, bottom, left and right).

Decide exactly where you want the turned-peg children to be located—on the boot and/or on the base slab—and bore the ½″-diameter

holes accordingly. Use a Forstner bit to achieve flat-bottomed holes, and plan on having the holes between ½ and ¾″ deep. Finally, drill out the pull-cord hole.

Assembling the Piece

Having made sure that all the parts are a good fit, glue the boot on the base slab. When the glue is dry, support the workpiece base and fasten with the countersunk screws. The drive shaft should be a smooth, contained, easy fit through the body of the boot, through the plywood sole, through the 1″-thick base slab, and through the under-axle base plate.

Use the pliers to cut the wire axle rods to length and to shape the Z-crank (Illus. 9, top). Test and adjust the movement of the crank, until the turning Z-crank sets the woman in motion (Illus. 9, bottom). When you have shaped the Z-crank and cut the two axles to length, run ⅛″-diameter axle holes halfway through the 1″ thickness of the wheels and fit the wheels to the axles with the resin glue. Finally, set the axles in their under-base slots, make sure that the Z-crank is located in the

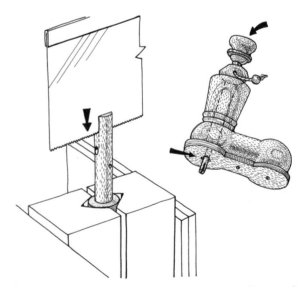

Illus. 8. Left: Use the straight saw to cut the crank-shaft location slot in the end of the drive shaft. Right: Slide the shaft down through the boot and secure with a wooden peg.

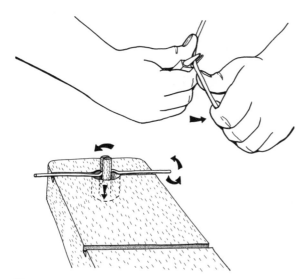

Illus. 9. Top: Bend the wire Z-crank to shape with a pair of pliers. Bottom: After testing the Z-crank, turn the toy over and put the Z-crank into the location slot and axle housing channel. Then twist the axle and check the movement.

drive-shaft slot, and screw the under-axle base plate into position.

Painting and Finishing

When you are pleased with the way the project fits together and functions, clear up all the dust and debris, and prepare your workshop for painting. Decide how far you want to strip the toy down in readiness for painting. Are you going to keep it assembled and simply be very careful, or are you going to unscrew and remove the various parts and paint them as separate units? Study the painting grid (Illus. 10) before you begin.

Bearing in mind that acrylics become dry to the touch in about 10 to 15 minutes, apply all the colors that make up the traditional design. You might have the base slab a bright red, the sole of the boot yellow, the wheels black, the boot left natural wood, the old woman's shawl red, black, and yellow, yellow for her bonnet, grey for her hair, and different-colored clothes for the children.

Finally, give the whole workpiece a couple of coats of varnish, attach the pull-cord, and this traditional action toy is ready to move.

Hints and Modifications

- If you have a good solid lathe, then you could eliminate the pre-lathe preparation of the wood and turn the square sections straight down to cylinders.
- When you are turning multiples—wheels, pegs, or whatever—it's always a good idea to turn a few extras. This way, you can choose the best of the bunch for well-matched sets.
- If you enjoy turning, you might make the children different sizes.
- You could further embellish the toy with, for example, painted lace holes and laces and windows on the boot.

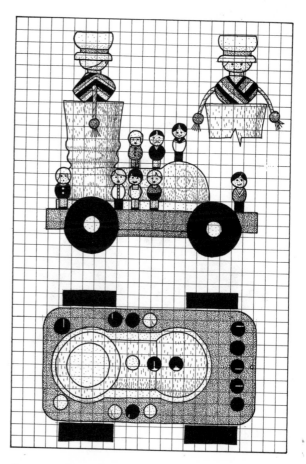

Illus. 10. Working-drawing painting grid. The scale is approximately three grid squares to 2".

139

14
A PULL-ALONG LADYBUG

A toy with ground ball-wheels and a friction-drive cradled ball body

Primary techniques: turning balls between centers, fretting, assembling, and painting

Children have a love-hate relationship with bugs—with all the spiders, earwigs, beetles, glowworms, and ants that hop, crawl, jump, and creep around our homes and gardens. But basically, most children enjoy having them around. They like to watch bugs feeding, build-ing their homes, laying eggs, and going about their daily rounds.

Of all the insects, the ladybug is one of the most useful. Did you know, for example, that the ladybug feeds on all the fat aphids that do so much damage in our fields, forests, and gardens?

This ladybug project is an intriguing toy that will give many hours of pleasure to children. In fact, so intriguing is this ladybug that, made at a slightly smaller scale, it could make a won-derful adult desk-top toy.

Design and Technique Considerations

Take a good look at the working drawings (Illus. 2) and see how, at a grid scale of four squares to 1″, the ladybug toy is 6″ long, 5″ high, and 5″ wide. Note how the four ground ball-wheels drive the large ball by means of direct friction. That is to say that the large removable ball is supported and cradled by the four contained ground ball-wheels so that, as the toy is pulled along, the revolving ball-wheels set the large ball in motion. Add to this five-ball movement the dramatic red-and-black imagery and the small, tight, carefully designed forms, and you have a really special and unusual toy.

Illus. 1. Project picture.

Tools and Materials

- A sheet of best-quality, ½″-thick, birch-faced multicore plywood at 4½ × 6″—which allows for waste.
- A 15″ length of 3 × 3″-square beech—for all the balls.
- Two 5″ lengths of ⅜″-diameter dowel—for the axles.
- A 12″ length of ½″-diameter dowel—for the ball-plug that is used during the turning.
- A pencil and ruler.
- A sheet each of work-out and tracing paper.
- A pair each of callipers and dividers.
- The use of a lathe.
- A good selection of wood-turning tools.
- A large four-jaw chuck to fit the lathe.
- A drill chuck to fit the tailstock.
- A long-shanked ½″-diameter spade or flat bit to fit the drill chuck.
- A hand drill with ⅜″ and ¼″ bits to fit.
- The use of a scroll saw—we use a Hegner.
- A pack of graded sandpapers.
- Cotton thread, wire hooks, pins, and a small cardboard box—to be used in the painting process.
- Acrylic paints in black and bright red.
- A couple of soft-haired brushes: a broad and a fine-point.
- A small quantity of white PVA wood glue.
- A can of clear beeswax polish.
- A length of soft ¼″-diameter rope—for the pull-cord.
- Workshop items such as water, old cloths, and disposable paint containers.

Setting Out and Making the Body and Side Plates

When you have studied the project picture (Illus. 1), the working drawings (Illus. 2), and all the details, and have a good understanding of the technique and tool implications of the project, clear your working area and set out all your tools and materials. Take the 6 × 4½″

sheet of ½″-thick plywood, and check it over just to make sure that it's free from warps, splits, stains, and delaminations. Trace off the design (Illus. 3, bottom) and then very carefully pencil-press-transfer the traced lines through to the working face of the plywood. Use a pencil, ruler, and punch to locate the position of the holes, and then mark all seven holes: the six axles holes and the single pull-cord hole. The axle-hole center-points need to be 2″ apart—on all three pairs of holes—in the axle plates and the main body. When you have established the position of the holes, double-check them against the working drawings, just to make sure that you haven't made a mistake. Using the ⅜″-diameter drill bit for the six axle holes and the ¼″-diameter bit for the single pull-cord hole, and making sure that the bit enters at right angles to the working face, bore out all seven holes. Support the workpiece on scrap wood so as to prevent the wood from splitting when the drill exits (Illus. 4, left).

With the holes running crisply and cleanly through the wood, use the scroll saw to cut out the three profiles: the main body and the two axle plates. You shouldn't have any problems, as long as you make sure, as you are sawing, to have the blade well-tensioned and running through the wood at 90° to the working face, to keep the wood moving smoothly so that the blade is always presented with the line of the next cut, and to keep a little to the waste side of the drawn line (Illus. 4, right). Finally, when you have achieved the three profiles, take the graded sandpapers and rub them down to a smooth, slightly round-edged finish.

Turning the Balls

Look back at Illus. 2 and see how there are five balls in all: the four ball-wheels at 1½″ in diameter and the single large body ball at 2½″ in diameter. On no account should the four ground ball-wheels be smaller than 1½″ in diameter. Note how the project allows for six small balls in all, with the best-matched four being used for the ball-wheels and the best of the other two for the pull-cord ball.

Having run through your safety pre-switch-on checklist (page 17), make sure that the lathe is in good condition and the four-jaw chuck is well fitted. Then mount the 15″ length of 3 × 3″-square beech in the chuck, and draw up the tailstock so that the wood is well secured. Once this is done, set the tool rest a little below lathe-center height, pin up the working drawings, and set out all your tools so that they are within reach.

Switch on the power, take the round-nosed gouge, and swiftly turn the wood down to a

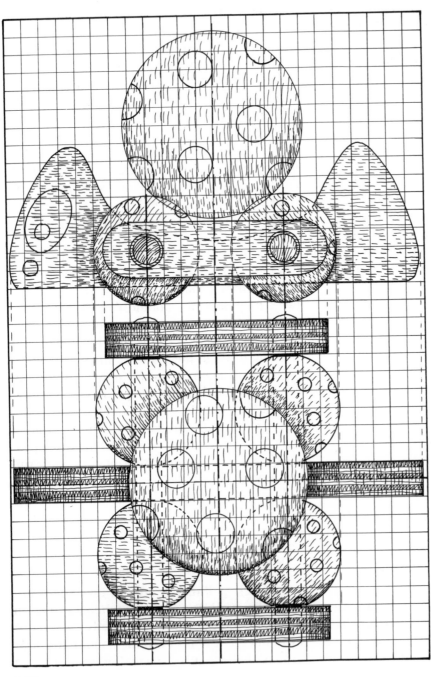

Illus. 2. Working drawings. The scale is four grid squares to 1″.

smooth 2½″-diameter cylinder. Now take the pencil, rule, and dividers and, working from left to right along the wood, mark all the step-offs that make up the design. If all is well, the step-offs should run from the chuck through to the tailstock in the order of 1″ to 2½″ and then alternately ¼″ and 1½″, until you get to the waste piece at the end of the wood (Illus.

5, top). Then take the parting tool and sink each of the ¼″ waste areas in to a depth of ⅝″ so as to leave a central core of waste that is 1¼″ in diameter. Next, turn each of the 1½″-wide step-offs down until they measure just a little over 1½″ in diameter.

When you have roughed out the primary turning, slide the tailstock back along the bed

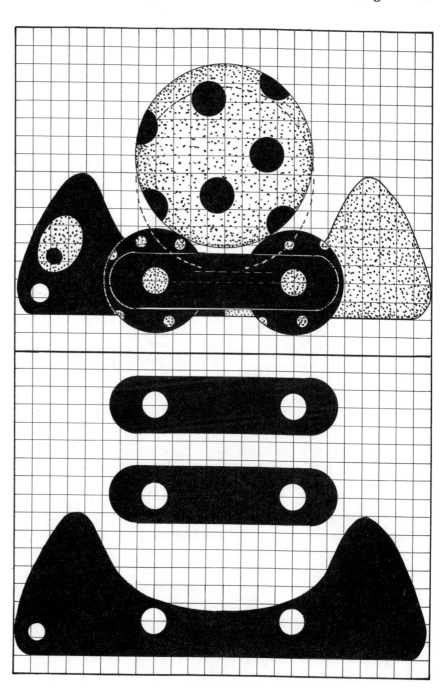

Illus. 3. Diagrammatic cutting grid and painting grid. The scale is four grid squares to 1″.

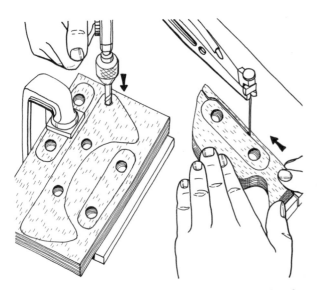

Illus. 4. Left: Slide a piece of scrap wood under the workpiece to prevent the wood from splitting when the drill exits. Right: Keep the wood moving so that the blade is always presented with the line of the next cut. Work a little to the waste side of the drawn line.

of the lathe and remove the tailstock morse center and replace it with the morse drill chuck. Fit the long-shanked ½"-diameter flat bit in the chuck. Now bring the drill bit up to the end of the turning, switch on the power, and carefully sink a ½"-diameter hole into the end of the wood to the full length of the drill shank. Having drilled the hole 3 to 4" into the wood, remove the drill and chuck, and refit the morse center. Take a length of ½"-diameter dowel, give it a swift sanding so as to reduce it very slightly in diameter, and then slide it into the end-of-wood hole that you have just drilled (Illus. 5, bottom) and saw it off level with the end of the turning. Reposition the tailstock center so that the workpiece is again supported at both ends.

Starting with the 1½"-diameter ball nearest the tailstock end of the lathe, take the skew chisel and turn the end waste down to a cone shape. When this is done, sink the waste on the other side of the ball by another ¼", pencil in the center-line of the ball (Illus. 6, top left), and reset the tool rest so that it is about ¼"

away from the workpiece. Now, still working with the skew chisel, turn down the shoulders of waste by pivoting the tool on the rest while at the same time running the cutting edge down into the waste and towards the dowel. Check the shape of the ball with a cardboard template (Illus. 6, top). Work with the grain, from pencil-marked peak to valley, that is, from the center of the ball, over and down in towards the waste at each side of the ball. Having achieved what you consider is a good ball shape, use the point of the skew chisel to turn the wood to a smooth finish and then carefully cut down towards the dowel (Illus. 6, top right). Ideally, the finished ball, or sphere, should still be marked with the center-line. When you reach a point when the ball is a free-turning bead, or ball, on the dowel, stop

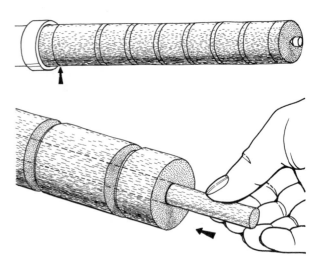

Illus. 5. Top: With pencil, ruler, and dividers, work from left to right, marking in all the step-offs that make up the design. Bottom: Reduce the dowel diameter so that it is a loose fit in the end-of-turning hole.

the lathe, wind back the tailstock, remove the first ball, remove the dowel, drill the hole deeper, replace the dowel, reposition the tailstock, and set to work turning the second ball. And so you continue, working along the wood until you have turned off six nearly identical

144

1½"-diameter balls. The only place that needs watching is when you come to about four balls away from the tailstock. Here, you will have to be careful not to run the central dowel hole into what will be the large body ball. All you need to do, as you approach the large ball, is to take measurements and to trim the central dowel to fit a shallower hole.

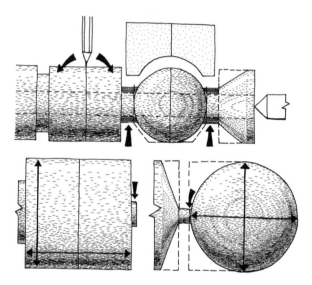

Illus. 6. Bottom left: Check with the callipers to make sure that the measurements—diameter and width—are equal, and then draw in a center-line. Top: Work with the grain from peak to valley, from the top of the ball down into the waste. When you are happy with the ball, turn off the final waste. Bottom right: Be careful not to reduce the wood at the arrow points.

When you have turned off the six ball-wheels, slide the tailstock well out of the way and use the pencil, ruler, and callipers to draw in the center-line of the large ball (Illus. 6, bottom left). Now, with the workpiece still securely mounted in the jaws of the chuck, turn off the waste from the tailstock end so as to complete one entire side of what will be the final 2½"-diameter body ball. Work just as you did with the small balls; that is, use the tool rest to pivot the tool. Make yourself a 2½"-diameter part-circle template out of thin card-

board, and use it to keep making checks. Remove as much waste as possible, until you are left with a small stalk of wood attaching the ball to the chuck (Illus. 6, bottom right). Finally, turn the ball to a smooth finish, cup it in one hand, and part it off from the lathe, and then use a scrap of sandpaper to rub the little stalk of waste down to a good finish.

Painting and Assembling

When you have made all the components—the four ball-wheels, the body ball, the body profile, and the axle plates—wipe them over with a dampened cloth and move them to the area that has been set aside for painting. With wire hooks, cotton, and pins, hang the balls and cutouts on a line in readiness for painting. The large ball needs to be supported in a card-board box so that it can be turned while being painted (Illus. 7, right). Set out your brushes and the red and black acrylic paints.

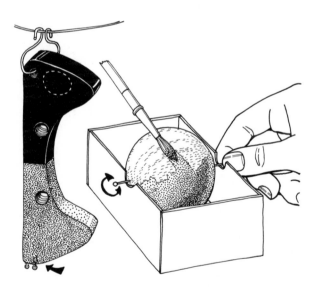

Illus. 7. Right: Support the large ball in a cardboard box, pivoted on two pins. The ball can now be painted on all sides. Left: Hang the body profile on a line from wire hooks. Paint it half-red and half-black, being careful to avoid drips and runs and getting paint in the axle holes.

Start by studying the painting grid (Illus. 3, top). Then paint the large areas of ground color: red for the large ball, black for the six small balls, black for the two axle plates, and half-black and half-red for the main body profile (Illus. 7, left). Make sure that you don't get any paint in the various axle holes. When the ground paint is dry, highlight the piece with the small dots that characterize the ladybug. Give the large red ball black dots, and give the small black balls red dots. Paint the eyes red with a black-dot pupil.

While the paint is drying, cut the two 4¾"-long, ⅜"-diameter axles to size, and rub the ends down to a slightly rounded, or domed, finish. Note: Allow for an extra 1/16" between moving parts.

When you are ready to assemble the toy, start by waxing and polishing all the components to a dull-sheen finish and then have a trial dry run. That is, take the four best-matched ball-wheels, the plywood profiles, and the two axle dowels, and slide them together and check for fit. The axles should be a tight friction-fit in the ⅜"-diameter body and plate holes, and a loose easy free-running fit through the ball-wheels. Aim to have the ends of the axles slightly proud so that they can be sanded to a nice half-round button shape. If all is well, dab a little glue on the axle centers, slide the axles in place through the body holes, slide the balls on the axles, dab a little glue on the ends of the axles, and slide the axle plates into position. Be very careful not to get the glue on the part of the axles that goes through the ball. Finally, when you have removed any blobs of glue, rewaxed any damaged areas, looped and knotted the cord in the ¼"-diameter hole, and knotted one of the small balls on the cord for a pull-hold, the ladybug is ready for its first ball-revolving trek around the playroom.

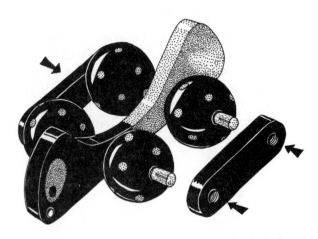

Illus. 8. Glue the axles in place in the body holes, and wipe away excess glue. Slide the free-running ball-wheels on the axles, glue the axle plates in place, and wipe away any unwanted glue.

Hints and Modifications

- Choose your wood with care. If you can't obtain beech, then ask a specialist supplier for another easy-to-turn wood, like cherry, sycamore, or apple.
- If you have a small lathe, you will have to cut the wood down to an octagonal section prior to turning. You may also need two turnings: one for the small balls, and one for the large ball.
- When you are choosing the plywood, be careful to avoid soft-heart varieties. Such sheet wood is very difficult to cut and almost impossible to bring to a good edge-finish.
- Although you can modify the design and have the large ball slightly larger, you can't much change the size of the four ground ball-wheels without totally changing the size of the other components.
- If the toy is to be given to a toy-sucking toddler, you might consider finishing it with varnish.

15
PULL-ALONG DANCING LADIES

A twirling, whirling friction-drive toy with dancing ladies

Primary techniques: turning between centers, beading, fretting, fitting with friction-drive wheels, and painting

Children get a real kick out of toys that move. If it's got wheels, then its sure to be a winner. Large fat wheels, wheels with spokes, wheels with plump black tires, wheels that turn, spin, twirl, and whirl—they are all good fun. But better still are wheeled toys that have a secondary movement. If, as the toy is being pulled along, the ground or drive wheels set some other part in motion, the toy is sure to be appreciated.

This toy scores on all counts. Not only are

Illus. 1. Project picture.

the four large wheels tracked and brightly painted, but, as the toy is pulled along, the dancing ladies slowly turn and whirl—and, what's more, in different directions.

The friction-drive mechanism is beautifully simple and direct. The fastened ground wheels turn the axles, the axles turn a couple of friction-drive wheels, and the wheels come into contact with the underside of the figures so as to set them pirouetting on their pivots.

Give this toy to a toddler, or even an adult, and watch him or her try to figure out how the ladies are able to turn in opposite directions. The special thing about this ingenious folk toy is that the workings are on view for all to see. Flip the toy over and slowly turn the wheels, and you will observe that the friction-drive wheels are mounted on opposite sides of the undercarriage. As the friction wheels rub on opposite sides of the pivoted ladies, they are set to twirling in different directions.

Design and Technique Considerations

Before you put tools to wood, take a good long look at the working drawings (Illus. 2 and 3) and see how the toy needs to be made and put together. Note the way all the forms have

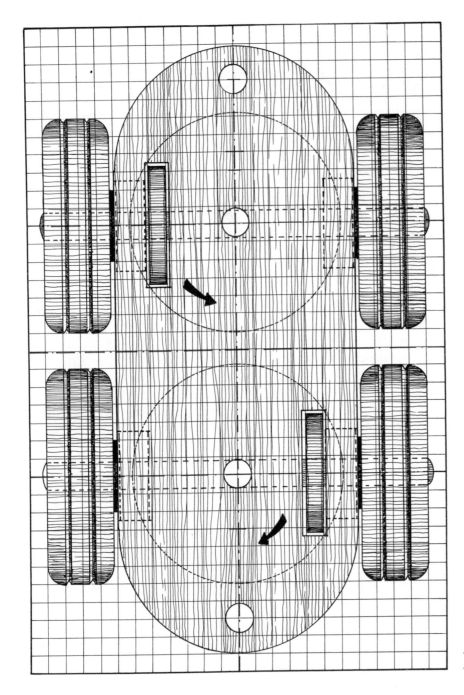

Illus. 2. Working drawing. The scale is four grid squares to 1".

been rounded for maximum safety: the round-edged wheels, the round ends to the chassis, and so on. Study the friction-drive mechanism and see how it is possible to modify the pivotal direction of one or both of the figures simply by having the drive wheel(s) on the other side of the toy. If you like the overall idea of the project but you want more ladies—perhaps three or four—all you do is make a longer plat-form, or chassis, and a set of ground wheels and a friction-drive wheel for each figure. Instead of the ladies, should you want sol-diers, animals, abstract shapes, or whatever, you just modify the design accordingly. How-ever, for maximum friction-drive efficiency, the figures do need to be wide and low rather than tall and spindly. Note, also, that the larger the diameter of the friction-drive wheel, the slower the figures will revolve.

Once you have a clear picture in your mind's eye of exactly how you want your toy to be—size, color, form, etc.—draw the designs up to size and finalize fitting and decoration details.

Tools and Materials

- A slab of ½"-thick beech that is 8½" long and 3½" wide—for the base.
- A 12" length of 3 × 3"-square wood—for the ground and friction-drive wheels, allowing for spares.
- A 14" length of 3 × 3"-square wood—for the two figures (this allows for a small amount for end wastage).
- A 6" length of ½ × ¾" wood—for the four axle bridge brackets.
- A selection of graded and paired colored wooden beads—for the arms, eight for each dancer.
- A 12" length of ⅜ to ½" dowel— for the two axles.
- The use of a lathe.
- The use of a workbench.
- Work-out and tracing paper.
- A good selection of turning tools.
- A pair each of dividers and callipers.
- A ¼"-wide mortise chisel.
- A straight saw.
- A hand drill with a selection of drill bits and a countersink.
- A coping saw.
- A quantity of PVA glue.
- A selection of broad and fine-point paint brushes.
- Acrylic paints in colors to suit.
- Two lengths of cord: fine for the arms and thick for the pull-cord.
- A can of clear high-gloss varnish.
- All the usual workshop items, such as old cloths, off-cuts, screws, a screwdriver, rubber bands, and so on.

Setting Out and Making the Chassis

When you have a clear image in your mind's eye and on paper of how you want the toy to be, and when you have fully considered all the working stages and procedures, check the wood over and spread it out on the workbench. You need four pieces of wood in all: the base slab, the 3 × 3"-square length for the two dancers, the 3 × 3"-square length for the wheels, and the slender length for the axle bridge brackets. Establish which length goes where, and label them with your pencil to avoid mix-ups.

Take the ½"-thick base slab, and use pencil, rule, and square to set out the total 8½ × 3½" shape, the end-to-end and side-to-side centerlines, the axle lines, and the position of the end-profile circles (Illus. 2). Label the slab "top" and "underside." Note that the circle centers should be on the end-to-end centerline, and set 1¾" along from each end of the slab. Adjust the compass to a radius of 1¾", and set each end of the slab out with a 3½"-diameter half-circle. Use a coping saw to clear away the small corners of waste.

Take pencil and ruler, and carefully establish the position of the two pull-cord holes on the "top" face of the slab and the position of the two pivotal holes on the "underside." The pull-cord holes are ½" along from the end of the base, and the pivot holes need to be on the axle-to-center-line crossover points. The pivotal holes must be set on the axle line at precisely 2½" along from each end of the base. The placement of the holes is important, so check them several times. Bore the pull-cord holes out with a ⅜ to ½" bit. Now flip the wood over so that the "underside" is uppermost, locate the two pivotal holes, and then, one hole at a time, run a ⅜"-wide blind countersink hole about ³⁄₁₆" into the wood, and follow it up with a ¼" hole that runs right through (Illus. 4, top). Do this with both pivot holes.

With pencil, ruler, and square, establish the precise position of the two drive-wheel slots.

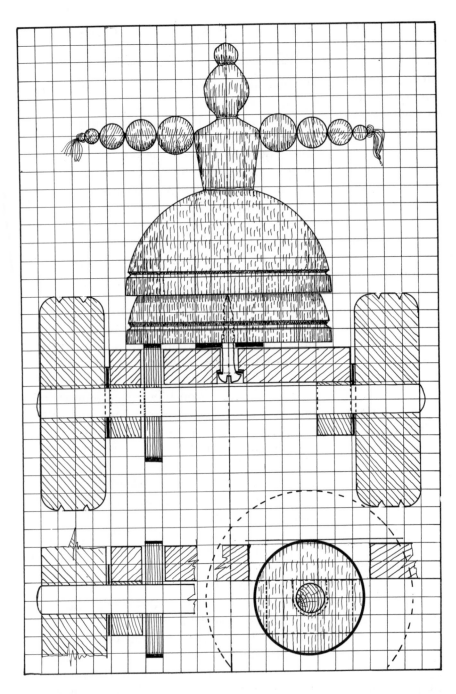

Illus. 3. Working drawings. The scale is four grid squares to 1".

Having noted that each slot needs to be slightly more than ¼″ wide, ½″ in from the side edge of the base, set at right angles to the axle, as well as 1¾″ long, set to work with the ¼″-wide chisel and run the mortise hole right through the wood (Illus. 4, bottom right). Finally, sand all cut edges to a smooth, slightly round-edged finish.

Making and Fitting the Bridge Bracket Axle Blocks

Having studied how the axle blocks are shaped and fitted (Illus. 3), take the length of ½ × ¾″ wood and draw out the four bridge-shaped profiles. Bear in mind, when you come to saw-

150

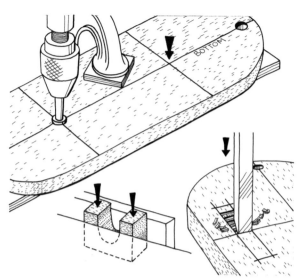

Illus. 4. Top: Run a ³/₈″-diameter blind countersink hole ³/₁₆″ down into the wood. Bottom right: Use the ¼″-wide mortise chisel to cut the mortise hole through the base. Bottom left: Drill ⅛″-diameter screw holes through at either side of the bridge bearings.

ing and shaping the little bridges, that it's important for the axle dowels to be a loose easy-turning fit. Run ⅛″-diameter screw holes through either side of the bridge shapes (Illus. 4, bottom left), and use the graded sandpapers to rub the wood down to a smooth round-edged finish.

When you have what you consider are four nicely finished blocks, set the base "underside" uppermost, set the bridge blocks astride the axle lines, and align them with both the edges of the base block and the drive-wheel mortises. Then screw the blocks in place, and check to be sure that the axles are a smooth easy-turning fit. Ideally, there should be a gap of about ¹/₁₆″ between all moving or turning faces; you might need to sand the axles or the bridges for an easy fit.

Turning the Ground and Friction-Drive Wheels

Look back at the working drawings (Illus. 2 and 3) and see how there are six wheels in all: the four ground wheels and the two drive wheels. Note how the ground wheels are wide and round-shouldered, while the drive wheels are sharp-edged and slender. The size and shape of the drive wheels is critical on two counts: In width and diameter, they must be an easy-turning fit in the base mortise slots, and the contact edge must be flat so as to achieve maximum contact with the underside of the pivotal figures.

When you have considered all possible variables that have to do with the wheels, take your 12″ length of 3 × 3″-square wood and check it over for possible faults and flaws. Establish the position of the end-centers by drawing crossed diagonals, and then mount the wood on the lathe. Position the tool rest so that it is as close as possible to the wood, and arrange all your tools so that they are comfortably close at hand.

When you have made sure that the lathe is in good condition, switch on the power and swiftly turn the wood down to a smooth 3″-diameter cylinder. It's all right if the cylinder is slightly less than 3″. Next, take the ruler and dividers, and set the wood out from left to right, that is, from the headstock through to the tailstock, first with a 1″ strip for waste and then with all the step-offs that go into making up the design. If you have a generous ½″-wide strip of waste between all wheels, you need five step-offs at 1″ wide for the ground wheels (Illus. 5, top) and three step-offs at ¼″ wide for the drive wheels. This arrangement allows for a spare for both types of wheels, just in case you make a mistake.

Having carefully established the width of the various step-offs, take the parting tool and sink the ½″-wide between-wheel waste in to a depth of about ¾″. Now take the skew chisel and, working from the middle of each wheel width and out and down around each shoulder, shape the wheel profile and the little V-section tread grooves (Illus. 5, bottom left). Aim to reduce the 1″-wide wheels ever so slightly, so as to finish up with wheels that are about ⅞″ wide. Turn the friction-drive wheels in like manner, only aim for wheels that are ¼″ wide and 1½″ in diameter. When you have brought all the wheels to a good finish, cut the between-wheel waste right down until you have a core of about ¼″, remove the workpiece from the lathe, and part off the separate wheels with a fine-toothed saw. Finally, establish the center-points, drill out the axle holes, and rub the sawn faces down with sandpaper (Illus. 5, bottom right).

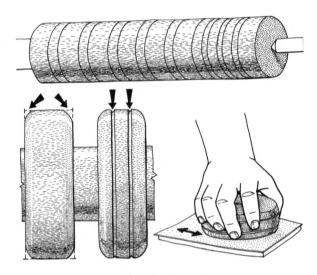

Illus. 5. Top: Step-off the five 1″-wide ground wheels and the three ¼″-wide drive wheels with ½″ waste between. Bottom left: Shape the wheel profile and the V-section tread grooves. Bottom right: Sand the sawn faces smooth by rubbing the wheels on a sanding block.

Turning the Figures

When you have spent time studying all the shapes that go into making up the figures, take the 14″ length of 3 × 3″-square wood and mount it on the lathe as already described. Switch on the power and turn the wood down to a 3″-diameter cylinder. Having seen how the two identical figures are worked as mirror images out of the single length of wood, make a marked-off cardboard or scrap-wood template, and use it to set the wood off with all the step-offs that make up the design. From left to center, the step-offs should be 2″ for headstock waste, ¾″ for the bottom skirt, 1½″ for the top skirt, ¾″ for the torso, ¼″ for the neck, ¾″ for the head, and ½″ for the hair bun. When you reach the hair-bun center-line, allow for ¼″ of waste. Then repeat the step-offs for the other figure, only this time have them set out in reverse order. When you come to using the template, hold it beside the turning cylinder and use the pencil to transfer the measurements through to the workpiece; then turn the template over and repeat the procedure for the second lady (Illus. 6).

Having established the position of all the reference points that go into making up the profile, take the parting tool or the skew chisel and sink depth guides at selected step-offs. Note: Leave the waste between the head and bun until the last possible moment; to remove it earlier would weaken the turning. So, for example, working from left to right along the wood, sink depth guides to mark the bottom of the figure, the top of the underskirt, the waist, the neck, and so on. It's all pretty straightforward, as long as you remember to sink the depth guides on or slightly to the waste side of the reference points. Bear in mind that the function of a depth guide is to establish the maximum depth of the profile at a given point.

With the depth guides well placed along the cylinder, take the skew chisel and start to turn away the waste. Working from left to right along the turning, and remembering to cut from high to low wood, first turn the two curves that make up the double skirt, then the waist, then the shoulders, and so on (Illus. 6, bottom). If, along the way, you want to create a slightly different profile—a more generous waist, a smaller head, or whatever—all you do is adjust the turning accordingly.

When you have achieved what you consider is a well-turned double-figure profile, skim the skew chisel over the wood to give it a super-smooth finish, drill out the arm holes, turn out the little area of waste between the head and bun, and part off. Note: You will have to be extra careful and support the wood at this stage.

Finally, rub the base of the underskirt down to a level finish.

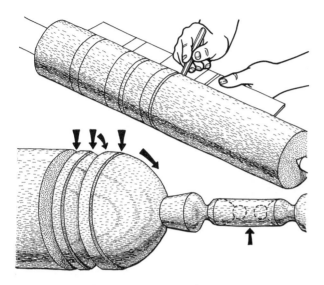

Illus. 6. Top: Hold the template against the turning and use it to transfer the measurements through to the workpiece. Reverse the template to mark off the second figure. Bottom: First turn the two curves that make up the double skirt, then the waist, shoulders, and neck, and lastly the fragile top-of-head ball. Then part off.

Painting, Assembling, and Finishing

Having cut and worked all the elements that make up the toy, study the painting grid (Illus. 7) and prepare your work area for painting. Set out your chosen colors, make sure that your brushes are clean, and rig up a line or rack so that the items can be supported while they are drying. When you come to painting, lay the colors on in single, thin, well-brushed coats, and give the workpiece a light sanding after the first coat. It's best to start with the large areas, and gradually work towards the small details. As for the choice of colors, you might have one lady with black hair and a yellow dress with red stripes, and the other lady with yellow hair and a red dress with yellow stripes. The base could be green, the wheels blue and yellow with red stripes, and so on; there are any number of exciting possibilities. With that said, I feel that toys are best painted with bold, bright primary and secondary colors rather than complex tertiaries. Children like strong colors—red, yellow, and blue—the brighter the better. Note: The axles and the drilled holes are best left unpainted.

When the paints are dry, then comes the enjoyable task of putting the toy together. Start by screwing the axle blocks, or mounts, in place on the underside of the chassis and making sure that the axles are a smooth-running fit. Have a trial placement of the wheels on the axles—the two ground wheels and a single friction-drive wheel on each axle. When you are satisfied with the placement and fit, carefully pencil in the placement on the axle, groove the wheel-to-axle mating surfaces with a saw or file to provide a key for the glue, slide the washers in place on the axles, and glue the friction-drive and the ground wheels in position. Glue a rubber band to the outer surface of the drive wheel.

When you have achieved a smooth-running fit of the wheels and axles, unscrew the axle mounting blocks, and screw the figures in position on the chassis. With a plastic or brass washer set between the underside of the figures and the base, run the screw up through a small washer and through the countersunk pivotal hole (Illus. 8, right). Replace the axle-and-wheels unit and see if the figure runs smoothly. You will likely need to keep fitting and adjusting the pivotal screw until the friction between the underside of the figure and the rubber-covered friction-drive wheel is just right. If everything is correct, when the toy is pulled or pushed along, the dancing ladies should turn around with an easy-spinning movement.

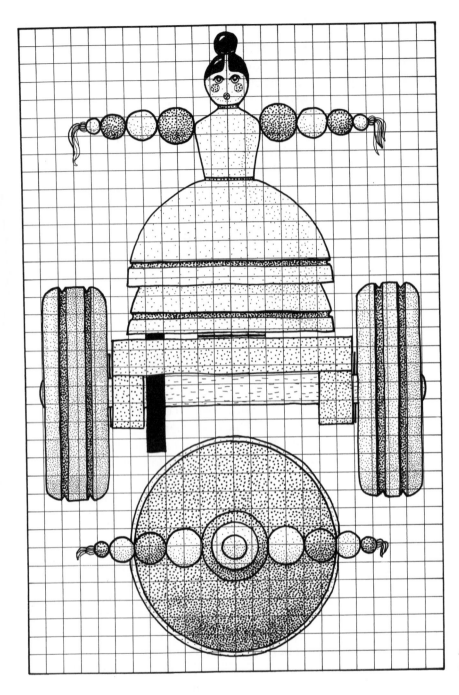

Illus. 7. Painting grid. The scale is four grid squares to 1".

Fitting the Pull-Cord, Tying the Triple-Strand Eye Splice, and Knotting the Beaded Arms

When you are ready to fit the pull-cord, loop it through the cord hole and tie an eye splice.

Start by threading the end loop through the pull-hole. Unwind the first 2″ of cord until you have three strands, and then very carefully wind a short length of fine twine around the cord so as to keep the twist from unravelling. Form a loop, thread the bottom strand through the "twist," and pull it through its full 2″. Take what is now the middle strand, and pass it through the next "twist" in like manner (Illus.

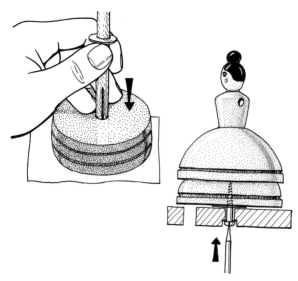

9, top right). Now, working on the other side of the splice, tuck the remaining strand and pass it through the next "twist" (Illus. 9, middle right). When this is done, repeat the procedure, and tuck each strand a second time along the "twist." Finish off by staggering the ends and cutting them at slightly different lengths. Now tap and roll the loop splice to make a tidy close fit (Illus. 9, bottom right).

Finally, thread up the beaded arms, secure the hand knots, and secure with a dab of glue (Illus. 9, left).

Illus. 8. Left: Working on a sheet of waxed paper, slide the washers in place on the axles and glue the wheels in position. Right: Adjust the pivotal screw on the underside of the figures until the friction between the figure and the wheel-drive is just right.

Hints and Modifications

- If you find wood turning difficult, you could modify the project by having shop-bought wheels, and carved-and-whittled figures.
- If you like the basic idea of the spinning movement but don't particularly care for the figures, you could modify the design by making brightly painted geometric or abstract forms instead.
- If you are using a large powerful lathe, the wood can be turned straight down from a square to a round section without pre-lathe preparation. But if you only have a small machine, it's best, prior to using the lathe, to prepare the wood by reducing it to an octagonal section.
- For smooth-running wheels, there needs to be a gap of about $1/16''$ between the wheels and the sides of the base. This can be achieved at the assembly stage by having cardboard spacer washers set on the axle, between the wheel and the base. Once the glue has dried, tear the cardboard washers away.
- Bearing in mind that this toy can be pulled from either end, another idea would be to have two cords—one at either end of the toy—and have a snap hook or shackle attached to one cord. Kids like hitching pull-along toys together to play towing games.

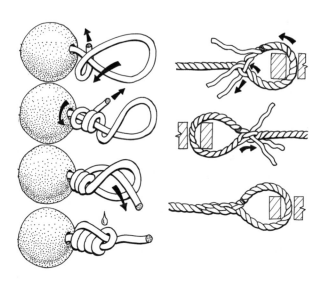

Illus. 9. Left, top to bottom: Securing the beaded arms. Make a figure-eight shape with the cord. Make three more passes. Thread the end through the first loop. Pull tight and hold with a dab of glue. Right, top to bottom: To make the splice, (top) pass the two strands through consecutive twists of the rope (middle), work the third strand from the other side and pass it through the next twist, and (bottom) complete the splice.

Metric Equivalents

INCHES TO MILLIMETRES AND CENTIMETRES

MM—millimetres   *CM—centimetres*

Inches	MM	CM	Inches	CM	Inches	CM
⅛	3	0.3	9	22.9	30	76.2
¼	6	0.6	10	25.4	31	78.7
⅜	10	1.0	11	27.9	32	81.3
½	13	1.3	12	30.5	33	83.8
⅝	16	1.6	13	33.0	34	86.4
¾	19	1.9	14	35.6	35	88.9
⅞	22	2.2	15	38.1	36	91.4
1	25	2.5	16	40.6	37	94.0
1¼	32	3.2	17	43.2	38	96.5
1½	38	3.8	18	45.7	39	99.1
1¾	44	4.4	19	48.3	40	101.6
2	51	5.1	20	50.8	41	104.1
2½	64	6.4	21	53.3	42	106.7
2	76	7.6	22	55.9	43	109.2
3½	89	8.9	23	58.4	44	111.8
4	102	10.2	24	61.0	45	114.3
4½	114	11.4	25	63.5	46	116.8
5	127	12.7	26	66.0	47	119.4
6	152	15.2	27	68.6	48	121.9
7	178	17.8	28	71.1	49	124.5
8	203	20.3	29	73.7	50	127.0

INDEX

About the Authors

A unique husband-and-wife team, Alan and Gill (for Gillian) Bridgewater are rapidly gaining an international reputation as producers of crafts books of the highest calibre. Gill does all the step-by-step illustrations, while Alan does the more technical illustrations, the research, and the writing.

Other Sterling books by the Bridgewaters are *Making Noah's Ark Toys in Wood, Folk Art Woodcarving: 823 Detailed Patterns*, and *Carving Totem Poles & Masks.*

The Bridgewaters have two children and live in a quayside captain's cottage in Cornwall, England.